INVENTING
KINDERGARTEN

INVENTING KINDERGARTEN

AN AUTOBIOGRAPHY
OF
FRIEDRICH FROEBEL

TRANSLATED AND ANNOTATED PY
EMILIE MICHAELIS
MEMBER OF THE COUNCIL OF THE FOREBEL SOCIETY, AND
MEMBER OF THE BOARD OF THE NATIONAL FROEBEL UNION

AND

H. KEATLEY MOORE
HON. TREASURER AND MEMBER OF THE COUNCIL
OF THE FROEBEL SOCIETY

Cosmo Publications
2009   New Delhi

INVENTING KINDERGARTEN

© Cosmo Publications, New Delhi
First published by COSMO 2009
First COSMO Paper back Edition 2007

ISBN 978-81-307-0870-6

Published by
COSMO PUBLICATIONS
for
GENESIS PUBLISHING PVT. LTD.
24-B, Ansari Road, Darya Ganj,
New Delhi-110 002,
INDIA

Printed and Bound in India

PREFACE TO THE FOURTH EDITION.

T is with some satisfaction that we are able to say that the corrections we have found it necessary to make in the text are very few and unimportant. We have taken this opportunity, however, to substitute for the original "Chronological Abstract" a much more complete and correct summary of the history of the movement than that which formerly accompanied our book. The recently published and most interesting "Reminiscences of Madame Luise Froebel" (Froebel's second wife, who happily still lives, at Hamburg) have been added in the present edition. We are favoured by the permission of the translator and of the publisher (Mr. George Philip) to use Miss Lyschinska's translation of these papers, which originally appeared in the early numbers of the English Froebelian journal, *Child Life*. A few slight verbal alterations have seemed advisable.

At the beginning of the present year the Croydon Kindergarten Company, in which both of us worked for so many years, and which has given us such a store of happy memories, ceased to exist, having honourably fulfilled its mission, and provided worthily for the continuation of its work. We can, therefore, no longer date from "The Croydon Kindergarten" as heretofore, but would request any corrections or observations with which readers may favour us to be sent to Mr. Moore, at 104, Bishopsgate Street Within, London, E.C.

EMILIE MICHAELIS.
H. KEATLEY MOORE.

11, NORLAND PLACE, NOTTING HILL.

PREFACE TO THE FIRST EDITION.

THE year 1882 was the centenary of Froebel's birth, and in the present "plentiful lack" of faithful translations of Froebel's own words we proposed to the Froebel Society to issue a translation of the "Education of Man," which we would undertake to make at our own cost, that the occasion might be marked in a manner worthy of the English branch of the Kindergarten movement. But various reasons prevented the Society from accepting our offer, and the lamentable deficiency still continues. We have therefore endeavoured to make a beginning by the present work, consisting of Froebel's own words done into English as faithfully as we know how to render them, and accompanied with any brief explanation of our own that may be essential to the clear understanding of the passages given. We have not attempted to rewrite our author, the better to suit the practical, clear-headed, common-sense English character, but have preferred simply to present him in an English dress with his national and personal peculiarities untouched.

In so doing we are quite aware that we have sacrificed interest, for in many passages, if not in most, a careful paraphrase of Froebel would be much more intelligible and pithy to English readers than a true rendering, since he probably possesses every fault of style except over-conciseness; but we feel that it is better to let Froebel speak for himself.

For the faithfulness of translation we hope our respective nationalities may have stood us in good stead. We would, however, add that a faithful translation is not a verbal translation. The translator should rather strive to write each sentence as the author would have written it in English.

Froebel's opinions, character, and work grow so directly out of his life, that we feel the best of his writing that a student of the Kindergarten system could begin with is the important autobiographical "Letter to the Duke of Meiningen," written in the year 1827, but never completed, and in all probability never sent to the sovereign whose name it bears. That this is the course Froebel would himself have preferred will, we think, become quickly apparent to the reader. Besides, in the boyhood and the earliest experiences of Froebel's life, we find the sources of his whole educational system. That other children might be better understood than he was, that other children might have the means to live the true child-life that was denied to himself, and that by their powers being directed into the right channels, these children might become a blessing to themselves and to others, was undoubtedly in great part the motive which induced Froebel to describe so fully all the circumstances of his peculiar childhood. We should undoubtedly have a clearer comprehension of many a great reformer if he had taken the trouble to write out at length the impressions of his life's dawn, as Froebel has done. In Froebel's particular case, moreover, it is evident that although his account of himself is unfinished, we fortunately possess all that is most important for the understanding of the origin of the Kindergarten system. After the "Letter to the Duke of Meiningen," we have placed the shorter account of his life which Froebel included in a letter to the philosopher Krause. A sketch of Barop's, which varies the point of view by regarding the whole movement more in its outer aspec than even Froebel himself is able to do, seemed to us also desirable to translate; and finally we have added also a carefully prepared "chronology" extended from Lange's list. Our translation is made from the edition of Froebel's works published by Dr. Wichard Lange at Berlin in 1862.

EMILIE MICHAELIS.

H. KEATLEY MOORE.

THE CROYDON KINDERGARTEN,

AUTOBIOGRAPHY OF FROEBEL.

(A LETTER TO THE DUKE OF MEININGEN.)

 WAS born at Oberweissbach, a village in the Thuringian Forest, in the small principality of Schwarzburg-Rudolstadt, on the 21st April, 1782. My father was the principal clergyman, or pastor, there.* (He died in 1802.) I was early initiated into the conflict of life amidst painful and narrowing circumstances; and ignorance of child-nature and insufficient education wrought their influence upon me. Soon after my birth my mother's health began to fail, and after nursing me nine months she died. This loss, a hard blow to me, influenced the whole environment and development of my being: I consider that my mother's death decided more or less the external circumstances of my whole life.

The cure of five thousand souls, scattered over six or seven villages, devolved solely on my father. This work, even to a man so active as my father, who was very conscientious in the fulfilment of his duty as minister, was all-absorbing; the more so since the custom of frequent services still prevailed. Besides all this, my father had undertaken to superintend the building of a large new church, which drew him more and more from his home and from his children.

I was left to the care of the servants; but they, profiting by my father's absorption in his work, left me, fortunately for me, to my brothers, who were somewhat older than myself.† This,

---

* Johann Jacob Froebel, father of Friedrich, belonged to the Old Lutheran Protestant Church.

† These were four (1) August, who went into business, and died young. (2) Christoph, a clergyman in Griesheim, who died . . . the typhus, which then overspread all central Germany, having broken . . . the over-crowded hospitals after the battle of Leipzig; he was the father of Julius, Karl, and

in addition to a circumstance of my later life, may have been the cause of that unswerving love for my family, and especially for my brothers, which has, to the present moment, been of the greatest importance to me in the conduct of my life. Although my father, for a village pastor, was unusually well informed— nay, even learned and experienced—and was an incessantly active man, yet in consequence of this separation from him during my earliest years I remained a stranger to him throughout my life ; and in this way I was as truly without a father as without a mother. Amidst such surroundings I reached my fourth year. My father then married again, and gave me a second mother. My soul must have felt deeply at this time the want of a mother's love,—of parental love,—for in this year occurs my first conscious- ness of self. I remember that I received my new mother over- flowing with feelings of simple and faithful child-love towards her. These sentiments made me happy, developed my nature, and strengthened me, because they were kindly received and recipro- cated by her. But this happiness did not endure. Soon my step-mother rejoiced in the possession of a son of her own ;* and then her love was not only withdrawn entirely from me and transferred to her own child, but I was treated with worse than indifference—by word and deed, I was made to feel an utter stranger.

I am obliged here to mention these circumstances, and to describe them so particularly, because in them I see the first cause of my early habit of introspection, my tendency to self- examination, and my early separation from companionship with other men. Soon after the birth of her own son, when I had

---

Theodor, the wish to benefit whom led their uncle Friedrich to begin his educational work in Griesheim in 1816. (3) Christian Ludwig, first a manu- facturer in Osterode, and then associated with Friedrich from 1820 onwards, —born 24th June, 1770, died 9th January, 1851. (4) Traugott, who studied medicine at Jena, became a medical man, and was burgomaster of Stadt-Ilm. Friedrich August Wilhelm himself was born on the 21st April, 1782, and died on the 21st June, 1852. He had no sisters.

* Karl Poppo Froebel, who became a teacher, and finally a publisher,— born 1786 ; died 25th March, 1824 : not to be confounded with his nephew, Karl, son of Christoph, now living in Edinburgh.

scarcely entered my boyhood, my step-mother ceased to use the sympathetic, heart-uniting "thou" in speaking to me, and began to address me in the third person, the most estranging of our forms of speech. And as in this mode of address the third person, "he," isolates the person addressed, it created a great chasm between my step-mother and me.* At the beginning of my boyhood, I already felt utterly lonely, and my soul was filled with grief.

Some coarse-minded people wished to make use of my sentiments and my mood at this time to set me against my step-mother, but my heart and mind turned with indignation from these persons, whom I thenceforth avoided, so far as I was able. Thus I became, at an early age, conscious of a nobler, purer, inner-life, and laid the foundation of that proper self-consciousness and moral pride which have accompanied me through life. Temptations returned from time to time, and each time took a more dangerous form : not only was I suspected as being capable of unworthy things, but base conduct was actually charged against me, and this in such a way as left no doubt of the impropriety of the suspicion and of the untruthfulness of the accusation. So it came to pass that in the first years of my boyhood I was perforce led to live to myself and in myself—and indeed to study my own being and inner consciousness, as opposed to external

---

* This needs explanation. In Germany, even by strangers, children are universally addressed in the second person singular, which carries with it a certain caressing sentiment. Grown persons would be addressed (except by members of their own family, or intimate friends) in the third person plural. Thus, if one met a child in the street, one might say, *Willst Du mit mir kommen ?* (Wilt thou come with me?) ; whereas to a grown person the proper form would be, *Wollen Sie mit mir kommen ?* (Will THEY—meaning, will YOU —come with me?). The mode of speech of which Froebel speaks here is now almost obsolete, and even in his day was only used to a person of markedly inferior position. Our sentence would run in this case, *Will Er mit mir kommen ?* (Will HE—meaning, will YOU, John or Thomas—come with me?), and carries with it a sort of contemptuous superciliousness, as if the person spoken to were beneath the dignity of a direct address. It is evident, therefore, that to a sensitive, self-torturing child like Froebel, being addressed in this manner would cause the keenest pain ; since, as he justly says, it has the effect, by the mere form of speech, of *isolating* the person addressed. Such a one is not to be considered as of our family, or even of our rank in life.

circumstances. My inward and my outward life were at that time, even during play and other occupations, my principal subjects for reflection and thought.

A notable influence upon the development and formation of my character was also exercised by the position of my parents' house. It was closely surrounded by other buildings, walls, hedges, and fences, and was further enclosed by an outer courtyard, a paddock, and a kitchen garden. Beyond these latter I was strictly forbidden to pass. The dwelling had no other outlook than on to the buildings to right and left, the big church in front, and at the back the sloping fields stretching up a high hill. For a long time I remained thus deprived of any distant view : but above me I saw the sky, clear and bright as we so often find it in the hill country ; and around me I felt the pure fresh breeze stirring. The impression which that clear sky and that pure air then made on me has remained ever since present to my mind. My perceptions were in this manner limited to only the nearest objects. Nature, with the world of plants and flowers, so far as I was able to see and understand her, early became an object of observation and reflection to me. I soon helped my father in his favourite occupation of gardening, and in this way received many permanent perceptions ; but the consciousness of the real life in nature only came to me further on, and I shall return to the point hereafter in the course of my narrative. Our domestic life at this time gave me much opportunity for occupation and reflection. Many alterations went on in our house ; both my parents were exceedingly active-minded, fond of order, and determined to improve their dwelling in every possible way. I had to help them according to my capacity, and soon perceived that I thereby gained strength and experience ; while through this growth of strength and experience my own games and occupations became of greater value to me.

But from my life in the open air amongst the objects of nature, and from the externals of domestic life, I must now turn to the inner aspects of my home and family.

My father was a theologian of the old school, who held knowledge and science in less estimation than faith; but yet he endeavoured to keep pace with the times. For this purpose he subscribed to the best periodicals he could obtain, and carefully examined what information they offered him. This helped not a little to elevate and enlighten the old-fashioned truly Christian life which reigned in our family. Morning and evening all its members gathered together, and even on Sunday as well, although on that day divine service would of course also call upon us to assemble for common religious worship. Zollikofer, Hermes, Marezoll, Sturm, and others, turned our thoughts, in those delightful hours of heavenly meditation, upon our innermost being, and served to quicken, unfold, and raise up the life of the soul within us. Thus my life was early brought under the influence of nature, of useful handiwork, and of religious feelings; or, as I prefer to say, the primitive and natural inclinations of every human being were even in my case also tenderly fostered in the germ. I must mention here, with reference to my ideas regarding the nature of man, to be treated of later, and as throwing light upon my professional and individual work, that at this time I used repeatedly, and with deep emotion, to resolve to try and be a good and brave man. As I have heard since, this firm inward resolution of mine was in flagrant contrast with my outward life. I was full of youthful energy and in high spirits, and did not always know how properly to moderate my vivacity. Through my want of restraint I got into all kinds of scrapes. Often, in my thoughtlessness, I would destroy the things I saw around me, in the endeavour to investigate and understand them.

My father was prevented by his manifold occupations from himself instructing me. Besides, he lost all further inclination to teach me, after the great trouble he found in teaching me to read —an art which came to me with great difficulty. As soon as I could read, therefore, I was sent to the public village school.

The position in which my father stood to the village schoolmasters, that is to say, to the Cantor,* and to the master of the girls' school, and his judgment of the value of their respective

---

* The Cantor would combine the duties of precentor (whence his title), leading the church singing and training the choristers, with those of the schoolmaster of the village boys' school. In large church-schools the Cantor is simply the choir-master. The great Bach was Cantor of the Thomas-Schule, Leipzig.

teaching, decided him to send me to the latter. This choice had a remarkable influence on the development of my inner nature, on account of the perfect neatness, quiet, intelligence, and order which reigned in the school ; nay, I may go further, and say the school was exactly suitable for such a child as I was. In proof of this I will describe my entrance into the school. At that time church and school generally stood in strict mutual relationship, and so it was in our case. The school children had their special places in church ; and not only were they obliged to attend church, but each child had to repeat to the teacher, at a special class held for the purpose every Monday, some passage of Scripture used by the minister in his sermon of the day before, as a proof of attention to the service. From these passages that one which seemed most suitable to children was then chosen for the little ones to master or to learn by heart, and for that purpose one of the bigger children had during the whole week, at certain times each day, to repeat the passage to the little children, sentence by sentence. The little ones, all standing up, had then to repeat the text sentence by sentence in like manner, until it was thoroughly imprinted on their memories.

I came into school on a Monday. The passage chosen for that week was, " Seek ye first the kingdom of God." I heard these words every day in the calm, serious, somewhat sing-song voices of the children, sometimes repeated by one child, sometimes by the whole number. And the text made an impression upon me such as none had ever done before and none ever did after. Indeed, this impression was so vigorous and permanent, that to this day every word spoken, with the special tone and expression then given to it, is still vivid in my mind. And yet that is now nearly forty years ago ! Perhaps even then the simple boy's heart felt that these words would be the foundation and the salvation of his life, bringing to him that conviction which was to become later on to the working and striving man a source of unconquerable courage, of unflinching, ever-ready, and cheerful self-sacrifice. In short, my introduction into that school was my birth into the higher spiritual life.

Here I break off my narrative to ask myself whether I dare venture to pause yet a little longer over this first period of my life. But this was the time when the buds began to unfold on my tree of life; this was the time when my heart found its pivot-point, and when first my inner life awoke. If, then, I succeed in giving an exact description of my early boyhood, I shall have provided an important aid to the right understanding of my life and work as a man. For that reason I venture to dwell at some inordinate length on this part of my life, and the more willingly since I can pass more quickly over later periods.

It often suggests itself to me, while thus reviewing and describing my life, just as it does with teaching and education—namely, that those things which are by most men thrown aside as common and unimportant are the very things which are, as I take it, of weightiest import. In my eyes, it is always a mistake to leave a gap in the rudimentary and fundamental part of a subject. Still I know one may exhaust the patience of a reader by touching on every minute detail, before he has been permitted to glance at the whole picture and to gather its scope and object. Therefore I beg your Highness * to pass over, at all events on the first reading, anything that may appear too long and too detailed.

Against standing rules, I was received in the girls' school, on account of the position of my father as pastor of the district. For the same reason I was placed, not with the pupils of my own age, but close to the teacher, which brought me among the elder girls. I joined in their lessons as far as I could. In two subjects I was quite able to do this. First, I could read the Bible with them; and, secondly, I had to learn line by line, instead of the little texts of the younger children already spoken of, the hymns for the following Sunday's service. Of these, two especially light up the gloomy lowering dawn of my early boyhood, like two brilliant stars. They are—"Schwing dich auf, mein Herz und Geist," and "Es kostet viel ein Christ zu sein." † These hymns were hymns of life to me. I found my own little life expressed

---

* It will be remembered that this letter is addressed to the Duke of Meiningen.

† "Arise, my heart and spirit," and "It costs one much (it is a difficult task) to be a Christian."

therein; and they took such a hold upon me that often in later years I have found strength and support in the message which they carried to my soul. My father's home life was in complete harmony with this discipline of the school. Although divine service was held twice on Sundays, I was but very seldom allowed to miss attending each service. I followed my father's sermons with great attention, partly because I thought I found in them many allusions to his own position, profession, and life. Looking back, I consider it of no slight importance that I used to hear the service from the vestry, because I was there separated from the congregation, and could the better keep my attention from wandering.

I have already mentioned that my father belonged to the old orthodox school of theology; and in consequence the language both of his hymns and of his sermons was mystical and symbolic —a style of speech which, in more than one sense, I should call a stone-language, because it requires an overwhelming power to burst its walls, and free from this outer shell the life contained within. But what the full strength of later life seems too weak to attain, is often accomplished by the living, life-awakening, and life-giving power of some simple, thoughtful young soul, by some young spirit first unfolding its wings, busily seeking everywhere for the causes and connections of all things. Even for such a youth, the treasure is to be gained only after long examination, inquiry, and reflection. If ever I found that for which I so longingly sought, then was I filled with exceeding joy

The surroundings amidst which I had grown up, especially those in which my first childhood was passed, had caused my senses to be much and early exercised. The pleasures of the senses were from the first, therefore, an object for the closest consideration with me. The results of this analysing and questioning habit of my early boyhood were perfectly clear and decisive, and, if not rendered into words, were yet firmly settled in my mind. I recognised that the transitory pleasures of the senses were without enduring and satisfying influence on man, and that they were therefore on no account to be pursued with too great eagerness. This conviction stamped and determined my whole being, just as my questioning examination and comparison of the inner with the outer world, and my study of their inter-connection, is now the basis of my whole future life. Unceasing self-contemplation, self-analysis, and self-education have been the fundamental characteristics of my life from the very first, and have remained so until these latest days.

To stir up, to animate, to awaken, and to strengthen, the pleasure and power of the human being to labour uninterruptedly at his own education, has become and always remained the fundamental principle and aim of my educational work.

Great was my joy when I believed I had proved completely to my own satisfaction that I was not destined to go to hell. The stony, oppressive dogmas of orthodox theology I very early explained away, perhaps assisted in this by two circumstances. Firstly, I heard these expressions used over and over again, from my habit of being present at the lessons given by my father in our own house, in preparation for confirmation. I heard them used also in all sorts of ways, so that my mind almost unconsciously constructed some sort of explanation of them. Secondly, I was often a mute witness of the strict way in which my father performed his pastoral duties, and of the frequent scenes between him and the many people who came to the parsonage to seek advice and consolation. I was thus again constantly attracted from the outer to the inner aspects of life. Life, with its inmost motives laid bare, passed before my eyes, with my father's comments pronounced upon it; and thing and word, act and symbol were thus perceived by me in their most vivid relationship. I saw the disjointed, heavy-laden, torn, inharmonious life of man as it appeared in this community of five thousand souls, before the watchful eyes of its earnest, severe pastor. Matrimonial and sexual circumstances especially were often the objects of my father's gravest condemnation and rebuke. The way in which he spoke about these matters showed me that they formed one of the most oppressive and difficult parts of human conduct; and, in my youth and innocence, I felt a deep pain and sorrow that man alone, among all creatures, should be doomed to these separations of sex, whereby the right path was made so difficult for him to find. I felt it a real necessity for the satisfaction of my heart and mind to reconcile this difficulty, and yet could find no way to do so.   How could I at that age, and in my position? But my eldest brother, who, like all my elder brothers, lived away from home, came to stay with us for a time; and one day, when I expressed my delight at seeing the purple threads of the hazel buds, he made me aware of a similar sexual difference in plants. Now was my spirit at rest.   I recognised that what had so weighed upon me was an institution spread over all nature, to which even the silent, beautiful race of flowers was submitted. From that time humanity and nature, the life of the soul and the life of the flower, were closely knit together in my mind; and I can still see my hazel buds, like angels, opening for me the great God's temple of Nature.

I now had what I needed: to the Church was added the Nature-Temple; to the religious Christian life, the life of Nature; to the passionate discord of human life the tranquil peace of the life of plants.   From that time it was as if I held the clue of Ariadne to guide me through the labyrinth of life.   An intimate communion with Nature for more than thirty years (although, indeed, often interrupted, sometimes for long intervals) has taught me that plants, especially trees, are a mirror, or rather a symbol, of human life in its highest spiritual relations; and I think one of the grandest and deepest fore-feelings that have ever emanated from the human soul, is before us when we read, in the Holy Scriptures, of a tree of knowledge of good and evil.   The whole of Nature teaches us to distinguish good from evil; even the world of crystals and stones—though not so vividly, calmly, clearly, and manifestly as the world of plants and flowers.   I said my hazel buds gave me the clue of Ariadne.   Many things grew clear to me: for instance, the earliest life and actions of our first parents in Paradise, and much connected therewith.

There are yet three points touching my inner life up to my tenth year, which, before I resume the narrative of my outer life, I should like to mention here.

The folly, superstition, and ignorance of men had dared to assume then, as they have done lately, that the world would soon come to an end.   My mind, however, remained perfectly tranquil, because I reasoned thus with myself firmly and definitely :—Mankind will not pass from the world, nor will the world itself pass away, until the human race has attained to that degree of perfection of which it is capable on earth. The earth, Nature in its narrowest sense, will not pass away, moreover, until men have attained a perfect insight into its essence. This idea has returned to me during my life in many a varied guise, and I have often been indebted to its influence for peace, firmness, perseverance, and courage.

Towards the end of this epoch, my eldest brother, already spoken of, was at the university, and studied theology.* Philosophic criticism was then beginning to elucidate certain Church dogmas. It was therefore not very surprising that father and son often differed in opinion. I remember that one day they had a violent dispute about religion and Church matters. My father stormed, and absolutely declined to yield; my brother, though naturally of a mild disposition, flushed deep-red with excitement; and he, too, could not abandon what he had recognised as true. I was present also on this as on many other occasions, an unobserved witness, and can still see father and son standing face to face in the conflict of opinion. I almost thought I understood something of the subject in dispute ; I felt as if I must side with my brother, but there seemed at the same time something in my father's view which indicated the possibility of a mutual understanding. Already I felt in a dim way that every illusion has a true side, which often leads men to cling to it with a desperate firmness. This conviction has become more and more confirmed in me the longer I have lived; and when at any time I have heard two men disputing for the truth's sake, I have found that the truth is usually to be learnt from both sides. Therefore I have never liked to take sides ; a fortunate thing for me.†

Another youthful experience which also had a decided influence in forming my cast of character, was the following :—There are certain oft-repeated demands made upon the members of our

---

* Christoph Froebel is here meant. He studied at the University of Jena.

† In this case Froebel's usually accurate judgment of his own character seems at fault ; his opinions being always most decided, even to the point of sometimes rendering him incapable of fairly appreciating the views of others.

Established Church ; such as, to enter upon the service of Christ, to show forth Christ in one's life, to follow Jesus, etc. These injunctions were brought home to me times without number through the zeal of my father as a teacher of others and a liver himself of a Christian life. When demands are made on a child which are in harmony with child nature, he knows no reluctance in fulfilling them; and as he receives them entirely and unreservedly, so also he complies with them entirely and unreservedly. That these demands were so often repeated convinced me of their intense importance; but I felt at the same time the difficulty, or indeed, as it seemed to me, the impossibility of fulfilling them. The inherent contradiction which I seemed to perceive herein threw me into great depression; but at last I arrived at the blessed conviction that human nature is such that it is not impossible for man to live the life of Jesus in its purity, and to show it forth to the world, if he will only take the right way towards it.

This thought, which, as often as it comes into my mind, carries me back even now to the scenes and surroundings of my boyhood, may have been not improbably amongst the last mental impressions of this period, and it may fitly close, therefore, the narrative of my mental development at this age. It became, later, the point whereon my whole life hinged.

From what I have said of my boyish inner life, it might be assumed that my outer life was a happy and peaceful one. Such an assumption would, however, not be correct. It seems as if it had always been my fate to represent and combine the hardest and sharpest contrasts. My outer life was really in complete contrast with my inner. I had grown up without a mother; my physical education had been neglected, and in consequence I had acquired many a bad habit. I always liked to be doing something or another, but in my clumsy way I made mistakes as to choice of materials, of time, and of place, and thus often incurred the severe displeasure of my parents. I felt this, being of a sensitive disposition, more keenly and more persistently than my parents; the more so as I felt myself generally to blame in form rather than in substance, and in my inmost heart I could see there was a point of view from whence my conduct would seem, in substance at all events, not altogether wrong, still less blameworthy. The motives assigned to my actions were not those which actuated me, so far as I could tell; and the consciousness of being mis-judged made me really what I had been believed to be before, a thoroughly naughty boy. Out of fear of punishment I hid even the most harmless actions, and when I was questioned I made untruthful answers.

In short, I was set down as wicked, and my father, who had not always time to investigate the justice of the accusations against me, remembered only the facts as they were represented to him. My neglected childhood called forth the ridicule of others; when playing with my step-brother, I was always, according to my mother, the cause of anything that went wrong. As the mind of my parents turned more and more away from me, so on my side my life became more and more separated from theirs; and I was abandoned to the society of people who, if my disposition had not been so thoroughly healthy, might have injured me even more than they did. I longed to escape from this unhappy state of things; and I considered my elder brothers fortunate in being all of them away from home. Just at this melancholy time came home my eldest brother. He appeared to me as an angel of deliverance, for he recognised amidst my many faults my better nature, and protected me against ill-treatment. He went away again after a short stay; but I felt that my soul was linked to his, thenceforth, down to its inmost depths; and indeed, after his death, this love of mine for him turned the whole course of my life.*

The boon was at last vouchsafed me, and that at my greatest need, to leave my father's house. Had it been otherwise, the flagrant contradiction between my outer and inner life must necessarily have developed the evil inclinations which had begun in earnest to fasten upon me. A new life entirely different from the former now opened before me. I was ten years and nine months old. But I pause yet another moment in the contempla-

---

* Froebel is alluding to his undertaking the education of his brother Chris-toph's sons, in November 1816, when he finally decided to devote his life to the cause of education.

tion of this period before I pass to its narration. In order to be clearly understood by your serene Highness, which is very necessary to me if I am to attain my object, I will compare, with your permission, my former life with my present. I shall endeavour to show how I trace the connection of my earlier and my later life; how my earlier life has proved for me the means of understanding my later; how, in general, my own individual life has become to me a key to the universal life, or, in short, to what I call the symbolic life and the perpetual, conditioned, and unbroken chain of existence.

Since, throughout the period which I have just described, my inner self, my life and being, my desires and endeavours, were not discerned by my parents, so is it with me now with regard to certain German Governments.* And just as my outward life then was imperfect and incomplete, through which incompleteness my inner life was misunderstood, so also now the imperfection and incompleteness of my establishment prevent people from discerning the true nature, the basis, the source, the aim and purpose, of my desires and endeavours, and from promoting them, after recognising their value, in a right princely and patriotic spirit.

The misapprehension, the oppression under which I suffered in my early years, prepared me to bear similar evils later on, and especially those which weigh upon me in the present circumstances of my life. And as I see my present private and public life and my destiny reflected in a part of my former life, just so do I read and trace the present universal life in my former individual life. Moreover, in the same way as I tried as child or boy to educate myself to be a worthy man according to those laws which God had implanted, unknown to me, within my nature, so now do I strive in the same way, according to the same laws, and

---

* At the time Froebel was writing this autobiographical letter (1827), and seeking thereby to enlist the Duke of Meiningen's sympathies in his work, in order to found a fresh institution at Helba, he was undergoing what was almost a persecution at Keilhau. All associations of progressive men were frowned upon as politically dangerous, and Keilhau, amongst the rest, was held in suspicion. Somewhat of this is seen in the interesting account by Barop further on ("Critical Moments at Keilhau").

by the same method, to educate the children of my country. That for which I strove as a boy, not yet conscious of any purpose, the human race now strives for with equal unconsciousness of purpose, but for all that none the less truly. The race is, however, surrounded by less favourable circumstances than those which influenced me in my boyhood.

Life in its great as well as in its small aspects, in humanity and the human race as well as in the individual (even though the individual man often wilfully mars his own existence)—life, in the present, the past, and the future, has always appeared to me as a great undivided whole, in which one thing is explained, is justified, is conditioned and urged forward by the other.

In order that, if it be possible, there should remain no obscurity whatever in my actions, thoughts, and life, I shall proceed to consider them all, down to the very latest event which has happened to me; that is, the writing-down of this statement of my life for your Highness. My life experience it is which urges me to do this; not any whim or caprice. Common worldly wisdom would challenge such a step if it were known; no one would desire to take it, no one would dare to take it. I dare it, and I do it, because my childhood has taught me that where for trust we find distrust, where for union we find division, where for belief we find doubt, there but sad fruit will come to the harvest, and a burdensome and narrow life alone can follow.

I return again to the narrative of the development of my inner and outer life.

A new existence now began for me, entirely opposed to that which I had hitherto led. An uncle on my mother's side came to visit us in this year; he was a gentle, affectionate man.* His appearance among us made a most agreeable impression upon me. This uncle, being a man of experience, may have noticed the adverse influences which surrounded me; for soon after his departure he begged my father by letter to turn me over to him entirely. My father readily consented, and towards the end of

---

* Herr Hoffmann, a clergyman, representing the State in Church matter for the district of Stadt-Ilm ; a post somewhat analogous to that of our arch-deacon.

the year 1792 I went to him. He had early lost both wife and child, and only his aged mother-in-law lived in his house with him. In my father's house severity reigned supreme ; here, on the contrary, mildness and kindness held sway. There I encountered mistrust ; here I was trusted. There I was under restraint ; here I had liberty. Hitherto I had hardly ever been with boys of my own age ; here I found forty schoolfellows, for I joined the upper class of the town school.*

The little town of Stadt-Ilm is situated in a somewhat wide valley, and on the banks of a small limpid stream.† My uncle's house had gardens attached, into which I could go if I liked ; but I was also at liberty to roam all over the neighbourhood, if only I obeyed the strict rule of the house to return punctually at the time appointed. Here I drank in fresh life-energy in long draughts ; for now the whole place was my playground, whereas formerly, at home, I had been limited to our own walls. I gained freedom of soul and strength of body.

The clergyman who taught us never interfered with our games, played at certain appointed playgrounds, and always with great fun and spirit. Deeply humiliating to me were the frequent slights I received in our play, arising from my being behind boys of my age in bodily strength, and more especially in agility ; and all my dash and daring could not replace the robust, steady strength, and the confident sureness of aim which my companions possessed. Happy fellows ! they had grown up in continual exercise of their youthful boyish strength. I felt myself exceedingly fortunate when I had at length got so far that my schoolfellows could tolerate me as a companion in their games. But whatever I accomplished in this respect by practice, by continual effort of will, and by the natural course of life, I always felt myself physically deficient in contrast with their uncramped boyish powers. Setting aside that which I had been robbed of by my previous education, my new

---

* Equal to an English middle-class school.

† The Ilm, flowing through Thuringia into the Saale. Oberweissbach is upon a tributary of the Schwarza, also flowing into the Saale. Weimar stands upon the Ilm, Jena upon the Saale.

life was vigorous and unfettered by external restraint; and they tell me I made good use of my opportunity. The world lay open before me, as far as I could grasp it. It may indeed be because my present life was as free and unconstrained as my former life had been cramped and constrained, anyhow the companions of my youth have reminded me of several incidents of that time which make me think that my good spirits led me to the borders of wildness and extravagance; although as a boy I considered my demeanour quieter by far than that of my companions of my own age. My communion with Nature, silent hitherto, now became freer and more animated. And as, at the same time, my uncle's house was full of peace and quiet contemplation, I was able as I grew up to develop that side of my character also; thus on every side my life became harmoniously balanced.

In two places, alike centres of education, I found myself as before quite at home, even though I was more frequently than ever the victim of absence of mind—I mean the church and the school. In the latter I especially enjoyed the hours devoted to religious instruction. As with my uncle himself, and with his life, so was it also with his sermons; they were gentle, mild and full of lovingkindness. I could follow them quite readily, and in the Monday repetition at school I was able to give a good account of them. But the religious instruction of our own schoolteacher responded best to my needs; all that I had worked out for myself was placed by him in a fuller light, and received from him a higher confirmation. Later in life, when I had grown to manhood, I spoke with my uncle on the excellence of this teaching, and he made reply that it was indeed very good, but was too philosophical and abstruse for those to whom it was addressed; "for thee," continued he, "it may have been well suited, since thou hadst already received such unusually good instruction from thy father." Let that be as it may, this teaching enlightened, animated, and warmed me,—nay, glowed within me till my heart was completely melted, especially when it touched upon the life, the work, and the character of Jesus. At this I would burst into tears, and the longings to lead in future a similar life took definite form, and wholly filled my soul. When I now hear tales of the ebullitions of my youthful spirit occurring in that period of my life, I cannot help thinking that they must have led superficial observers to the erroneous opinion that the monitions and teachings of religion swept over my spirit without leaving a trace of their passage. And yet how wrongly would such observers have judged the true state of my inner life!

The subjects best taught in the school of Stadt-Ilm were reading, writing, arithmetic, and religion. Latin was miserably taught, and still worse learnt. Here, as in so many similar schools, the teaching utterly lacked the elucidation of first principles. The time spent on Latin was therefore not wasted upon me, in so far that I learnt from it that such a method of teaching could bear no fruit among the scholars. Arithmetic was a very favourite study of mine; and as I also received private tuition in this subject, my progress was so rapid that I came to equal my teacher both in theory and practice, although his attainments were by no means despicable. But how astonished was I when, in my twenty-third year, I first went to Yverdon, and found I could not solve the questions there being set to the scholars! This was one of the experiences which prepossessed me so keenly in favour of Pestalozzi's method of teaching, and decided me to begin arithmetic myself from the very beginning over again, according to his system. But more of this later.

In physical geography we repeated our tasks parrot-wise, speaking much and knowing nothing; for the teaching on this subject had not the very least connection with real life, nor had it any actuality for us, although at the same time we could rightly name our little specks and patches of colour on the map. I received private tuition in this subject also. My teacher wished to advance further with me; he took me to England. I could find no connection between that country and the place and country in which I dwelt myself, so that of this instruction also I retained but little. As for actual instruction in German, it was not to be thought of; but we received directions in letter-writing and in spelling. I do not know with what study the teaching of spelling was connected, but I think it was not connected with any; it hovered in the air. I had lessons, furthermore, in singing and in pianoforte playing, but without result. I merely mention all this now, in order to be able to refer to it later on.

My life the whole time of my stay with my uncle had three aspects : the religious life developing and building up my moral being; the external life made up of boyish play, into which I threw my whole energy; and the life of thought quietly showing itself within my uncle's peaceful home. To this last influence also I yielded myself with equal earnestness, and felt no suspicion of the apparent contradiction which my outward life exhibited to such a mood. Like my school-fellows, I lived without control; as far as I saw or felt, I was untrammelled; and yet I do not call to mind that any of us ever committed a seriously culpable action.

Here I am obliged to mention something which as an educationist I can by no means pass lightly by. We received instruction from two schoolmasters : one was pedantic and rigid; the other, more especially our class-teacher (*conrector*), was large-hearted and free. The first never had any influence over his class; the second could do whatever he pleased with us, and if he had but set his mind to it, or perhaps if he had been aware of his power, he might have done some thoroughly good sound work with his class. In the little town of Stadt-Ilm were two ministers, both ephors * of the school. My uncle, the principal minister, was mild, gentle, and kind-hearted, impressive in daily life as in his sacred office or in the pulpit; the other minister was rigid even to sternness, frequently scolding and ordering us about. The first led us with a glance. A word from him, and surely few were so brutish as to refuse that word admittance to their heart. The long exhortations of the other went, for the most part, over our heads, leaving no trace behind. Like my father, my uncle was a true shepherd of his flock; but a gentle lovingkindness to all mankind reigned in him. My father was moved by the conviction of the rectitude of his actions; he was earnest and severe. Both have been dead over twenty years; but how different is the spirit they have left behind amongst their congregations. Here, they are glad at being released from so strict a control, and, if I am rightly informed, unbridled license

---

* Superintendents. The *ephors* of ancient Sparta amongst their duties had that of the superintendence of education, whence the German title.

has sprung up amongst them; there, the little town raises itself to higher and ever higher prosperity, and all things are made to serve towards mental culture, as well as towards a right citizen-like business activity. I permit myself this digression, because these results were paralleled as a life-experience in my own life.

In this manner I lived, up to my confirmation; all but a few weeks, that is, which I spent at my parents' house during the long holidays. Here, too, everything seemed to take a gentler turn, and the domestic, thrifty activity which filled the place, and always struck me anew in my periodical visits home, wrought upon me with most beneficial effect. The copper-plate engravings in my father's library were the first things I sought out, especially those representing scenes in the history of the world. A table showing our (German) alphabet in its relations with many others made a surprising impression upon me. It enabled me to recognise the connection and the derivation of our letters from the old Phœnician characters. This gave me a dim conception of the inner connection of all those languages of which, as my brother had studied and was still studying them, I often heard, and saw in print. Especially the Greek language lost much of its strangeness in my eyes, now that I could recognise its characters in the German alphabet. All this, however, had no immediate consequence in my life; these things, as echoes from my youth, produced their effect upon me at a later time.

At this time, too, I read all sorts of boys' books. The story of Samuel Lawill impressed me most vividly; I, too, longed for such a ring, which by its warning pressure on my finger could hinder my hand from effecting unworthy purposes, and I was very angry with the youthful owner of the ring in the story, who threw it away in irritation because it pressed him right hard at a moment when he wished to commit a passionate deed.*

My confirmation, and the preparation for it, all conducted by

---

* The story is now forgotten, but its nature is sufficiently indicated in the text.

my uncle, was over. I had received from it the most impressive and the most far-reaching influence in my whole life, and all my life-threads found in it their point of union and repose. I had now to be prepared for some business calling, and the question was raised, for which ? That I should not study at the university had already been decided long before by the express determination of my step-mother. For since two of my brothers * had devoted themselves to study, she feared that the further additional expense would be too heavy a burden upon my father's means. It may be that this intention had already influenced and limited my whole course of instruction; and probably only the little narrow circle of future business aims had been considered; the eye had not looked upon the boy as a future man. Possibly from this cause I was kept so little to Latin; it was enough if I learnt, as our mode of expression ran, to "state a *Casus*" (that is, to decline a noun). From my own experience it was thus shown to me how eminently injurious it is in education and in instruction to consider only a certain circle of future activities or a certain rank in life. The wearisome old-fashioned education *ad hoc* (that is, for some one special purpose) has always left many a noble power of man's nature unawakened.

A career in our country frequently chosen by the worthiest and most anxious parents for their sons is that of a post in the Treasury and Exchequer. Aspirants to such a post have two means of entering and two starting-points in this career; either they become a clerk to one of the minor officials in the Treasury or Exchequer, or the personal servant of one of the highest officials. As my knowledge of writing and figures seemed to my father satisfactory and sufficient for such a post, and as he knew well that it might lead, not merely to a life free from pecuniary cares, but even to wealth and fortune, he chose this career as mine. But the minor Treasury official who might have found employment for such a young man, showed various reasons why he could not or would not as yet receive me as a clerk. There was something in my nature which revolted against the second mode I have mentioned of entering this career; something which I never afterwards experienced, but which at the time absolutely

---

* Christoph and Traugott.

prevented me from choosing such a mode of starting in my future profession, and that in spite of the most alluring hopes that were held out to me. My father meant well and honestly by me, but fate ruled it against him. Strangely enough, it happened that in my later capacity of schoolmaster, I became the educator and teacher of two of the nephews of that very man into whose service my father had meant to have sent me; and I hope to God that I have been of greater service to that family by filling the heart and brain of these young people with good and useful notions than if I had brushed the clothes and shoes of their uncle, and spread his table with savoury dishes. In the latter case, very likely an externally easy and happy existence might have been mine, whereas now I wage a constant fight with cares and difficulties.

Suffice it to say, this career was closed to me; a second was proposed by my mother, but from this my father delivered me by expressing a decided disapproval.

My own desires and inclinations were now at last consulted. I wanted to be an agriculturist in the full meaning of the word; for I loved mountain, field, and forest; and I heard also that to learn anything solid in this occupation one must be well acquainted with geometry and land-surveying. From what I had learnt of the latter by snatches now and then, the prospect of knowing more about it delighted me much; and I cared not whether I began with forestry, with farming, or with geometry and land-surveying. My father tried to find a position for me; but the farmers asked too high a premium. Just at this time he became acquainted with a forester who had also a considerable reputation as land-surveyor and valuer. They soon came to terms, and I was apprenticed to this man for two years, to learn forestry, valuing, geometry, and land-surveying. I was a little over fifteen years old when I became an apprentice to the forester, on Midsummer Day, 1797.

It was two days' journey from my home to the forester's, for his district was not in our country. The man often gave me proofs of his thorough and many-sided knowledge; but he did not understand the art of conveying his knowledge to others, especially because what he knew he had acquired only by dint of actual experience.*　Further, some work of timber-floating † with which he had been entrusted hindered him from devoting to me the stipulated time necessary for my instruction.

As soon as I saw this quite clearly, my own activity of mind urged me to make use of the really excellent books on forestry and geometry which I found lying to my hand. I also made acquaintance with the doctor of a little town near by, who studied natural science for his amusement; and this friend lent me books on botany, through which I learnt also about other plants than just those of the forest. A great deal of my time during the absence of the forester (when I was left quite to myself) I devoted to making a sort of map of the neighbourhood I lived in; but botany was my special occupation. My life as forester's apprentice was a four-fold one: firstly, there was the homelier and more practical side of life; then the life spent with Nature, especially forest-nature; then also a life of the study, devoted to work at mathematics and languages; and lastly, the time spent in gaining a knowledge of plants. My chosen profession and the other circumstances of my position might have brought me into contact with many kinds of men; but nevertheless my life remained retired and solitary. My religious church life now changed to a religious communion with Nature, and in the last half-year I lived entirely amongst and with my plants, which drew me towards them with fascination, notwithstanding that as yet I had no sense of the inner life of the plant world. Collecting and drying specimens of plants was a work I prosecuted with the greatest care. Altogether this time of my life was devoted in many various ways to self-education, self-instruction, and moral advancement. Especially did I love to indulge my old habit of self-observation and introspection.

---

* In Germany a *Forstmann*, or forester, if he has studied forest cultivation in a School of Forestry, rises eventually to the position of supervisor of forests (*Forst-meister*). The forester who does not study remains in the inferior position.

† In the German State forests, the timber, when cut down, is frequently not transported by road, but is made to slide down the mountain-sides by timber-shoots into the streams or rivers; it is then made up into rafts, and so floated down to its destination.

I must mention yet another event of the greatest importance from the point of view of my inner life. An hour's walk from where I then lived was a small country town. A company of strolling actors arrived there, and played in the prince's castle in the town. After I had seen one of their performances, hardly any of those which followed passed without my attendance. These performances made a deep and lively impression upon me, and this the more that I felt as if my soul at last received nourishment for which it had long hungered. The impressions thus gained lasted so much the longer, and had so much the greater influence on my self-culture, in that after each performance my hour's walk home by dark or in the starlight allowed me to recapitulate what I had heard, and so to digest the meaning of the play. I remember especially how deeply a performance of Iffland's *Huntsmen* moved me, and how it inspired me with firm moral resolutions, which I imprinted deep in my mind under the light of the stars. My interest in the play made me seek acquaintance with the actors, and especially with one of them, an earnest young man who attracted my attention, and to whom I spoke about his profession. I congratulated him on being a member of such a company, able to call up such ennobling sentiments in the human soul ; perhaps even expressed a wish that I could become a member of such a company. Then the honest fellow described the profession of an actor as a brilliant, deceitful misery, and confessed to me that he had been only forced by necessity to adopt this profession, and that he was soon about to abandon it. Once again I learned by this to divide cause from effect, internal from external things. My visits to the play brought upon me a most unpleasant experience, for my father, when I spoke to him without concealment of my playgoing, reproached me very bitterly for it. He looked upon my conduct as deserving the highest punishment, which was in absolute contradiction with my own view ; for I placed the benefit I had derived from my attendance at the play side by side with what I had received by my attendance at church, and expressed something of the kind to my father. As often happened in later life, so also on this occasion it was my eldest brother who was the mediator between my father and myself.

On Midsummer Day 1799 my apprenticeship came to an end. The forester, who could now have made my practical knowledge of service to himself, wished to keep me another year. But I had by this time acquired higher views; I wished to study mathematics and botany more thoroughly, and I was not to be kept back from my purpose. When my apprenticeship was over I left him, and returned to my father's house.

My master knew well that he had not done his duty towards me, and with this probably humiliating consciousness before him, and in spite of the thoroughly satisfactory testimonial that he gave me, he committed a very mean action against me. He did not know anything about my private study; for instance, my completely working through some elementary mathematical books, which I had found myself quite well able to understand. Besides, he was dissatisfied that I would not stay another year with him. He therefore sent a letter to my father, in which he complained bitterly of my conduct, and shifted the blame of my ignorance of my calling entirely on to my shoulders. This letter actually arrived at home before I did; and my father sent it on to my eldest brother, who was minister in a village through which I had to pass on my way home. Soon after I reached my brother's house he communicated to me the contents of this inculpatory letter. I cleared myself by exposing the unconscientious behaviour of my master, and by showing my private work. I then wrote a reply to my master, clearly refuting all his accusations, and exhibiting on the other hand his behaviour towards me; and with this I satisfied my father and my brother. But the latter reproached me for having suffered wrongdoing so long without complaint. To that I gave the simple answer, that my father, at the beginning of my apprenticeship, had told me not to come to him with any complaint, as I should never be listened to, but should be considered as wrong beforehand. My brother, who knew my father's severity and his views on such points, was silent. But my mother saw in one declaration of the forester the confirmation of her own opinion about me. The forester declared, that if ever anything was made of me, the same good fortune might be told of the first-comer without further trouble, and my mother assented heartily to his opinion.

Thus disappeared once more the light, the sunshine, which had gladdened me with its warmth, especially in the more recent part of my life. The wings of my mind, which had begun to flutter of themselves, were again bound, and my life once more appeared all cold and harsh before me. Then it happened that my father had to send some money to my brother (Traugott), who was studying medicine in Jena. The matter pressed ; so, as I had nothing to do, it was decided that I should be the messenger.

When I reached Jena I was seized by the stirring intellectual life of the place, and I longed to remain there a little time. Eight weeks of the summer half-year's session of 1799 yet remained. My brother wrote to my father that I could fill that time usefully and profitably in Jena, and in consequence of this letter I was permitted to stay. I took lessons in map and plan-drawing, and I devoted all the time I had to the work. At Michaelmas I went home with my brother, and my step-mother observed that I could now fairly say I had passed through the university. But I thought differently ; my intelligence and my soul had been stimulated in many ways, and I expressed my wish to my father to be allowed to study finance there, thus returning to my previous career. My father was willing to give his permission if I could tell him how to find the means. I possessed a very small property inherited from my mother, but I thought it would be insufficient. However, after having conferred with my brother, I talked it over with my father. I was still a minor, and therefore had to ask the consent of my trustee to realise my property ; but as soon as I had obtained this I went as a student to Jena, in 1799. I was then seventeen years and a half old.

A testimonial from my father attesting my capacity for the curriculum procured me matriculation without difficulty. My matriculation certificate called me a student of philosophy, which seemed very strange, because I had set before me as the object of my studies practical knowledge ; and as to philosophy, of which I had so often heard, I had formed a very high idea of it. The word made a great impression upon my dreamy, easily-excited, and receptive nature. Although the impression disappeared almost as soon as conceived, it gave, however, higher and unexpected relations to my studies.

The lectures I heard were only those which promised to be useful in the career I had now again embraced. I heard lectures on applied mathematics, arithmetic, algebra, geometry, mineralogy, botany, natural history, physics, chemistry, accounts, cultivation of forest trees and management of forests, architecture, house-building, and land-surveying. I continued topographical drawing. I heard nothing purely theoretical except mathematics; and of philosophical teaching and thought I learnt only so much as the intercourse of university life brought with it; but it was precisely through this intercourse that I received in various ways a many-sided intellectual impulse. I usually grasped what had been taught; the more thoroughly since, through my previous life, I had become well acquainted with the principal subjects, and already knew their relation to practical work.

Some of the lectures were almost easy for me—for instance, those on mathematics. I have always been able to perceive with ease and pleasure relations of geometrical figures and of planes; so that it seemed inexplicable to me that every farmer should not be equally capable of understanding them. This I had said before to my brother, who tried to give me an explanation; but I did not yet grasp it. I had expected I don't know exactly what, but certainly something higher, something grandiose; very likely I had expected something with more life in it. The mathematical course, therefore, at first seemed to me unimportant; but later on I found that I, also, could not follow every detail. However, I did not think much of this, because I readily understood the general meaning, and I said to myself that particular cases would not cause me any mental fatigue if I found it necessary to learn them.

The lectures of my excellent teacher were not so useful to me as they might have been, if I could have seen in the course of instruction and in its progress somewhat more of necessary connection and less of arbitrary arrangement. This want of necessary connection was the reason of the immediate dislike I always took to every course of instruction. I felt it even in pure mathematics, still more was it the case in applied mathematics, and most of all in experimental physics. Here it seemed to me as if everything were arranged in arbitrary series, so that from the very first

I found this study a fatigue. The experiments failed to arrest my attention. I desired and sought after some inner connection between the phenomena, deduced from and explained by some simple root principles. But that was the very point withheld from me. Mathematical demonstrations came like halting messengers ; they only became clear to the mind's eye when the truth to be demonstrated lay before me already in all its living strength. On the other hand, my attention was riveted by the study of gravitation, of force, of weight, which were living things to me, because of their evident relation to actual facts.

In mechanics (natural philosophy) I could not understand why so many of the so-called "mechanical powers" were assumed, and why several of them were not reduced to cases of the inclined plane.

In mineralogy my previous education had left many gaps unfilled, especially as regards the powers of observation. I was fond of mineral specimens, and gave myself much trouble to comprehend their several properties ; but in consequence of my defective preparation I found insuperable difficulties in my way, and perceived thereby that neglect is neither quickly nor lightly to be repaired. The most assiduous practice in observation failed to make my sight so quick and so accurate as it ought to have been for my purpose. At that time I failed to apprehend the fact of my deficient quickness of sight ; it ought to have taught me much, but I was not prepared to learn the lesson.

Chemistry fascinated me. The excellent teacher (Göttling) always demonstrated the true connection of the phenomena under consideration ; and the theory of chemical affinity took strong hold upon me.

Note-taking at these lectures was a thing I never thought of doing ; for that which I understood forthwith became a part of me, and that which I failed to understand seemed to me not worth writing down. I have often felt sorry for it since. But as regards this point, I have always had through my whole life the perfectly clear conviction that when I had mastered a whole subject in its intimate relations I could go back upon, and then understand, details which at the time of hearing had been unintelligible to me.

In botany I had a clear-sighted, kind-hearted teacher (Batsch). His natural system of botany* gave me great satisfaction, although I had always a painful perception of how much still remained for him to classify. However, my view of Nature as one whole became by his means substantially clearer, and my love for the observation of Nature in detail became more animated. I shall always think of him with gratitude. He was also my teacher in natural history. Two principles that he enunciated seized upon me with special force, and seemed to me valid. The first was the conception of the mutual relationship of all animals, extending like a network in all directions; and the second was that the skeleton or bony framework of fishes, birds, and men was one and the same in plan, and that the skeleton of man should be considered as the fundamental type which Nature strove to produce even in the lower forms of creation.† I was always highly delighted with his expositions, for they suggested ideas to me which bore fruit both in my intelligence and in my emotional nature. Invariably, whenever I grasped the inter-connection and unity of phenomena, I felt the longings of my spirit and of my soul were fulfilled.

I easily understood the other courses I attended, and was able to take a comprehensive glance over the subjects of which they treated. I had seen building going on, and had myself assisted in building, in planting, etc.; here, therefore, I could take notes, and write complete and satisfactory memoranda of the lectures.

My stay in Jena had taught me much; by no means so much as it ought to have taught me, but yet I had won for myself

---

* Jussieu's natural system of botany may possibly be here alluded to. The celebrated "Genera Plantarum" appeared in 1798, and Froebel was at Jena in 1799. On the other hand, A. J. G. Batsch, Froebel's teacher, professor at the university since 1789, had published in 1787-8 his "Anleitung zur Kentniss und Geschichte der Pflanzen," 2 vols. We have not seen this work. Batsch also published an "Introduction to the Study of Natural History," which reached a second edition in 1805.

† In justice to Froebel and his teacher, it must be remembered that the theory of evolution was not as yet formed, and that those who dimly sought after some explanation of the uniformity of the vertebrate plan, which they observed, were but all too likely to be led astray.

a standpoint, both subjective and objective. I could already perceive únity in diversity, the correlation of forces, the inter-connection of all living things, life in matter, and the principles of physics and biology.

One thing more I have to bring forward from this period. Up till now my life had met with no sympathetic recognition other than the esteem which I had enjoyed of the country physician during my apprenticeship—he who encouraged me to study natural science, and smoothed away for me many a difficulty. But now such sympathy was destined to offer itself as a means of education and improvement. For there were in Jena just then two scientific associations, one for natural history and botany, the other for mineralogy, as it was then called. Many of the young students, who had shown living interest and done active work in natural science, were invited to become members by the President, and this elevating pleasure was also offered to me. At the moment I certainly possessed few qualifications for member-ship; the most I could say was that my faculty for arranging and classifying might be made of some use in the Natural History Society, and this, indeed, actually came to pass. Although my admission to this society had no great effect upon my later life, because it was dissolved at the death of its founder, and I did not keep up my acquaintance with the other members afterwards, yet it awakened that yearning towards higher scientific knowledge which now began to make itself forcibly felt within me.

During my residence at the university I lived in a very retired and economical way; my imperfect education, my disposition, and the state of my purse alike contributing to this. I seldom appeared at places of public resort, and in my reserved way I made my brother (Traugott) my only companion ; he was studying medicine in Jena during the first year of my residence there.*

---

* The text (Lange, Berlin, 1862) says *meinen ältesten Bruder*, that is, "my eldest brother ;" but this is quite an error, whether of Froebel or of Herr Lange we cannot at present say. As we have already said in a footnote on p. 3, August was the eldest brother of Friedrich, and Christoph was the eldest then living. Traugott, who was at Jena with Friedrich, was his next older brother, youngest of the first family, except only Friedrich himself. It is Traugott who is meant in this passage.

The theatre alone, of which I was still passionately fond, I visited now and then. In the second year of this first studentship, in spite of my quiet life, I found myself in an awkward position. It began, indeed, with my entrance into the university, but did not come to a head till my third half-year. When I went to the university, my father gave me a bank draft for a small amount to cover my expenses, not only for the first half-year, but for the entire residence, I think. My brother, who, as I said, was with me at Jena for the first year, wished me to lend him part of my allowance, all of which I did not then require, whereas he was for the moment in difficulties. He hoped soon to be able to repay me the money. I gladly gave him the greater part of my little draft; but unfortunately I could not get the money back, and therefore found myself in greater and greater difficulties. My position became terribly urgent; my small allowance had come to an end by the close of the first year, but I could not bring myself to leave the university, especially now that a yearning for scientific knowledge had seized me, and I hoped for great things from my studies. Besides, I thought that my father might be induced to support me at the university another half-year.

My father would hear nothing of this so far as he was concerned; and my trustee would not agree to the conditions offered by my father (to cover an advance); so I had to pay the penalty of their obstinacy.

Towards the end of my third half-year the urgency of my difficulties increased. I owed the keeper of an eating-house (for meals) thirty thalers, if I am not mistaken. As this man had caused me to be summoned for payment several times before the Senate of the University, and I had never been able to pay, and as he had even addressed my father, only to receive from him a sharp refusal to entertain the matter, I was threatened with imprisonment in the case of longer default of payment. And I actually had to submit to this punishment. My step-mother inflamed the displeasure of my father, and rejoiced at his inflexibility. My trustee, who still had the disposal of some property of mine, could have helped me, but did not, because the letter of the law was against any interference from his side. Each one hoped by the continuance of my sorry plight to break the stubbornness of the other. I served as scapegoat to the caprices of the obstinate couple, and languished as such nine weeks long in the university prison at Jena.* At last my father consented to advance me money on my formally abandoning, before the university board, all claim on his property in the shape of inheritance ; and so, in the end, I got free.

In spite of the gloom into which my position as a prisoner plunged me, the time of my arrest was not utterly barren. My late endeavours towards scientific knowledge had made me more and more conscious of my need of a solid foundation in my knowledge of Latin ; therefore I now tried to supply deficiencies to the extent of my ability, and with the help of a friend. It was extremely hard to me, this working my way through the dead and fragmentary teaching of an elementary grammar. It always seemed to me as if the mere outer acquisition of a language could but little help forward my true inner desire for knowledge, which was deeply in earnest, and was the result of my own free choice. But wherever the knowledge of language linked itself to definite external impressions, and I was able to perceive its connection with facts, as, for instance, in the scientific nomenclature of botany, I could quickly make myself master of it. This peculiarity of mind passed by me unnoticed at the time ; I knew and understood too little, nay, indeed, almost nothing of myself as yet, even as regards the actions of my every-day life.

A second occupation of this prison period was the preparation of an exercise (or academical thesis) in geometry, which I undertook that I might the sooner obtain an independent position in some profession.

Thirdly, I studied Winckelmann's "Letters on Art." Through them some germs of higher artistic feeling may have been awakened within me ; for I examined the engravings which the work contains with intense delight. I could quite perceive the glow of pleasure that they aroused, but at the time I took little

---

* "In carcer ;" that is, in the prison of the university, where in the last resort students who fail to comply with university regulations are confined. The "carcer" still exists in German universities. It has of course nothing to do with the ordinary prison of the town.

account of this influence, and indeed the feeling for art altogether was late in developing itself in me. When I now glance over the earlier and later, the greater and smaller, artistic emotions which have swayed me, and observe their source and direction, I see that it was with arts (sculpture as well as music) as it was with languages—I never succeeded in accomplishing the outward acquisition of them : yet I now feel vividly that I, too, might have been capable of something in art had I had an artistic education.

Further, there came into my hands, during the time of my imprisonment, a bad translation of an abridgment of the Zendavesta. The discovery [in these ancient Persian Scriptures] of similar life-truths to our own, and yet coupled with a quite separate religious standpoint from ours, aroused my attention, and gave some feeling of universality to my life and thought ; this, however, disappeared as quickly as it had come.

By the beginning of the summer term in 1801 I was at length set free from arrest. I at once left Jena and my academical career, and returned to my father's house. I was just nineteen years old. It was but natural that I should enter my parents' house with heavy heart, overclouded soul, and oppressed mind. But spring warmed and awakened all nature once more, and recalled to life, too, my slumbering desire for better things.

As yet I had busied myself but little with German literature, and the names of Schiller, Goethe, Wieland, and the rest I now, for the first time, began to learn. In this, too, it was with me as in so many other things ; any mental influence that came before me I had either to fully interweave with my inner life, or else altogether to forego its acquisition.

With this peculiarity of temperament, I could master only a rather restricted amount of mental material. My father's library was once more ransacked. I found not much that was of any use to me, for it contained chiefly theological works ; but I seized with the greatest enjoyment on a book which had come out some ten years before in Gotha, a general view of all the sciences and fine arts in their various ramifications, with a short sketch of the object of the several sciences and of the literature of each department. The arrangement was based upon the usual division of the faculties, but it served to give me a general outlook, long desired, over the whole of human knowledge, and I was right glad to have found this " Mappe du monde littéraire "—for that was its title. I resolved to turn this book to the best advantage I could, and set about putting my resolution into practice. In order to make a collection of comprehensive extracts of scientific matters from the several periodicals received by my father (who shared for that purpose in a joint subscription with other preachers and educated people), I had already begun a sort of diary. The form of this journal was shapeless—everything was put down as it came, one thing after the other; and thereby the use of it all was rendered very inconvenient. Now, however, I perceived the value of division according to a settled plan, and soon hit upon a scheme of procedure.

I aimed at collecting all that seemed worthy to be known, all that was necessary for cultured men in general, and for myself in my own calling in particular; and this rich treasure was to be brought out under favourable circumstances, or whenever need was, from its storehouse. Also I desired to acquire a general idea of those subjects which the craving for knowledge, growing ever more and more sharp within my soul, was always urging me thoroughly to work through over again. I felt happy in my work; and I had already been chained to my task for several days, from early morning till late at night, in my little distant chamber with its iron-barred windows, when my father suddenly and unexpectedly walked into the room. He looked over what I had done, and remarked the quantity of paper used over it, which indeed was not small. Upon this cursory inspection he held my work for a foolish waste of time and paper; and it would have been all over with my labour of love for that time, if my brother (Christoph), who had so often stood as protector by my side, had not just then been on a visit with us. He had become the minister of a place which lay a few hours' journey from Ober-weissbach, and at this moment was staying with my parents. My father at once told him of what he considered my useless, if not indeed injurious occupation; but my brother saw it differently. I ventured, therefore, to continue, with the silent permission of my father. And indeed the work proved of actual service to me, for it brought a certain order, breadth, and firmness into my ideas which had the most beneficial effect upon me.

My father now strove to procure me a settled position in my chosen calling; or at all events to provide some active work which would bring me into nearer connection with it. And for this purpose a fortunate opportunity soon offered. Some of my father's relatives had property in the district of Hildburghausen, managed by a steward. The friendly footing on which my father stood with these relatives permitted me to study practical farming under this steward. There I took part in all the ordinary farming occupations. These, however, did not attract me greatly, and I ought to have at once discovered what an unsuitable career I had chosen, if I had but understood my own nature.

The thing that most painfully occupied my mind at this time was the absence of cordial understanding between me and my father. At the same time I could not help esteeming and honouring him. Notwithstanding his advanced age he was still as strong and as healthy in body as in mind, penetrating in speech and counsel, vigorous in fulfilment and actual work, earnest, nay, hard, in address. He had a firm, strong will, and at the same time was filled with noble, self-sacrificing endeavour. He never shirked skirmish nor battle in the cause of what he deemed the better part; he carried his pen into action, as a soldier carries his sword, for the true, the good, and the right. I saw that my father was growing old and was drawing near the grave, and it made me sorry to feel that I was yet a stranger to such a father. I loved him, and felt how much good resulted from that love; so I took the resolution to write to my father, and by letter to show him my true nature, so far as I could understand myself. Long did I revolve this letter in my mind; never did I feel strength nor courage to write it. Meanwhile a letter called me back home in November, after I had been some months engaged on the estate. I was called upon to help my father, now quite weak and almost bedridden; at all events I could assist him in his correspondence. Family and other cares and the activities of life absorbed my whole time. What I meant to have done in my letter now happily became possible in speech from man to man, in glances from eye to eye. My father was occupied by cares for my future prospects up till the end. He died in February 1802. May his enlightened spirit look down full of peace and blessing upon me as I write ; may he now be content with that son who so loved him !

I now stood in every respect my own master, and might decide the direction of my future life for myself, according to the circumstances which lay around me. With this intention I once more left the paternal roof at Easter, to undertake the post of clerk in the Office of Woods and Forests which formed one part of the general administration (divided into Treasury, Woods and Forests, and Tithe departments) of the as yet episcopal territory of Bamberg.* My district lay amidst unusual and lovely scenery ; my duties were light, and when they were over I was free to roam in the neighbourhood, now doubly beautiful in the springtime, to live out my life in freedom, and gain strength for mind and soul.

Thus once again I lived much out of doors and in companionship with Nature. My chief was proud of the possession of a considerable library, of which I made good use ; and in this manner many of the publications then issuing from the press, and treating of matters connected with the occupation which I had chosen, passed through my hands, as well as those on other subjects. I was especially attracted by some volumes which contained aphorisms, thoughts, and observations on conduct, selected from ancient and modern writers and thinkers. My character grew upon and entwined itself around these aphorisms, which I could easily glance over, and as easily retain, and, more than all, which I could weave into my own life and thoughts, and by which I could examine my conduct. I made extracts of those which were in closest accord with my inner life, and bore them always about my person.

Amidst these surroundings my life contained many elements of growth. Although my chief, as well as his family, was a strong Roman Catholic, he chose a (Protestant) private tutor recommended to him by Professor Carus. This gentleman had many

---

* The Prince-Bishop of Bamberg shared in the general Napoleonic earthquake. The domain of the bishopric went to Bavaria ultimately, the title alone remaining to the Church.

excellent qualities, so that we soon became great friends. We had also both of us the pleasure of being acquainted with some highly-cultured people, the families of the physician, of the minister, and of the schoolmaster in the neighbouring Protestant village, which was as yet still a fief of the Empire.* My friend the tutor was a young man quite out of the common, with an actively inquiring mind ; especially fond of making plans for wide-stretching travels, and comprehensive schemes of education. Our intercourse and our life together were very confidential and open, for the subjects he cared for were those dear to me ; but we were of diametrically opposite natures. He was a man of scholastic training, and I had been deficiently educated. He was a youth who had plunged into strife with the world and society ; my thought was how to live in peace with myself and all men. Besides, our outward lives bore such different aspects that a truly intimate friendship could not exist between us. Nevertheless our very contrasts bound us more closely together than we deemed.

Practical land-surveying at this time chiefly interested me, for it at once satisfied my love for out-of-doors life, and fully occupied my intelligence. But the everlasting scribbling which now fell to my share I could not long endure, in spite of my otherwise pleasant life.

Early in the spring of 1803 I left my situation and went to Bamberg, feeling sure that the political changes by which Bamberg had been transferred to Bavaria, and the general survey of the district which was therefore in contemplation, would immediately provide me with a sphere of work suited to my capabilities. My expectations were not falsified. In pursuance of my plan I introduced myself to the land-surveyors in Bamberg, and at once received employment from one of them. He had had considerable surveys in hand, and was still engaged upon them. As I showed some proficiency in mapping, he entrusted me with the preparation of the necessary maps which accompanied the surveys. This

---

* Shared the fate of the Bamberg possessions, and of many other principalities and small domains at that time existent ; namely, absorption under the Napoleonic *régime* into the neighbouring States. This went to Bavaria ; see the text, later on.

kept me employed for some time on work sufficiently remunera-
tive for my needs.

Of course the question in hand with the new Government was
the appointment of land-surveyors, and those who were resident
in the town were invited to send in maps of Bamberg as specimens
of their work. Through the instruction I had enjoyed in my
youth I was not unacquainted with such work. I therefore took
pleasure in drawing a map, which I sent in. My work was
approved, and I received something for it; but being a stranger,
inexperienced, and young, and having hardly taken the best way
towards my purposed aim, I obtained no appointment.

After I had finished the work I have mentioned the survey of a
small private property was put into my hands to carry out. From
this engagement ensued consequences which were most important
for me. I note only one point here. One of the joint owners of this
property was a young doctor of philosophy, who leaned towards
the new school of Schelling. It could hardly be expected but that
we should talk over things which stirred our mental life, and so
it came about that he lent me Schelling's " Bruno, oder über die
Welt-seele " * to read. What I read in that book moved me pro-
foundly, and I thought I really understood it. The friendly young
fellow, not much older than myself—we had already met in Jena,
—saw the lively interest I was taking in the book, and, in fact, I
talked it over with him many a time. One day, after we had been
to see an important picture-gallery together, he addressed me in
these words, which from his mouth sounded startlingly strange,
and which at the time seemed to me inexplicable :—

" Guard yourself against philosophy ; she leads you towards
doubt and darkness. Devote yourself to art, which gives life,
peace, and joy."

It is true I retained the young man's words, but I could not understand them, for I regarded philosophy as a necessary part of the
life of mankind, and could not grasp the notion that one could be
verging towards darkness and doubt when one calmly investigated
the inner life. Art, on the other hand, lay much further from me
than philosophy ; for except a profound enjoyment in works of art

---

* Bruno, or concerning the Over-Soul.

(for which I could give no clear reason), no glimmering of an active æsthetic sense had yet dawned upon me. This remark of my friend the doctor's called my attention to myself, however, and to my life and its aim, and made me aware of two very different and widely separate systems of life.

My friend, the tutor of the Government official under whom I had served at Bamberg, had in the meantime left his situation. He told me before leaving that he had it in his mind to go to Frankfurt, and thence into France. I saw his departure with regret, little dreaming that life would in a few years bring us together again, and that he would indirectly decide my future career. But, as it so often happens in life, parting in this instance but led up to meeting, and meeting to parting.

The occurrences I have named had little result upon my outward life, which for the time ran its peaceful course. I pass over many circumstances important to the uplifting and development of my character and my moral life, and come at once to the close of my stay in Bamberg.

I had now once more earnestly to turn my attention to procuring certain and settled employment. In truth, as regarded my future, I stood quite alone. I had no one to lend me a helping hand, so I made up my mind to go forward, trusting only in God and destiny. I determined to seek for a situation by means of the *Allgemeine Anzeiger der Deutschen*,* a paper then very much read, and I thought it would be good to send in to the editor, as a proof of my assertions of competency, an architectural design, and also a specimen of my work in practical surveying, together with explanations of both of them. As soon as my plan was fully conceived I set to work at it. For the architectural sketch I chose a design of a nobleman's country mansion, with the surrounding outbuildings. When I had finished it, with very few professional appliances to help me, it contained a complete working out of all the various necessary plans, and as a critical test of its accuracy and suitability to the proposed scale of dimensions, I added a statement of all the particulars and conditions involved in it. For the land-surveying I chose a table of measurements compiled from

---

* "General Intelligencer of the German people."

the map I had previously drawn, which I carried through under certain arbitrary assumptions. These works, together with my advertisement, I sent in 1803 to the office of the paper I have mentioned, with the request that the editor, after reading my testimonials and inspecting my work, would add a few confirmatory words as to my qualifications. Work and testimonials alike were to the satisfaction of the editor, and my request for an editorial comment was granted. I received several offers, each one containing something tempting about it. It was difficult to make a choice, but at last I decided to accept a position offered me as private secretary to the President and Privy-Councillor Von Dewitz, of Mecklenburg-Strelitz, at this time resident on one of his estates, Gross-Milchow.

Amongst the other offers was one from Privy-Councillor Von Voldersdorf, who was looking out for an accountant for his estates in the Oberpfalz.* This situation did not suit me so well as the other, but I accepted a proposition to fill up the time till the arrangements for the other post had been completed, by going down to these estates of Herr Von Voldersdorf, and bringing into order, according to a certain specified plan, the heavy accounts of his steward, which were at this time much in arrear. I set off for the Oberpfalz in the first days of 1804. But I was soon called away to Mecklenburg to the situation at Gross-Milchow which I had definitively chosen, and in the raw, frightfully severe wintertime of February I journeyed thither by the mail-coach. Yet, short as had been my stay in the Oberpfalz, and continual and uninterrupted as had been my labour in order that I might get through the work I had undertaken, the time I spent in Bavaria yielded me much that was instructive. The men, ingenuous, lively young fellows from Saxony and Prussia, received me very kindly, and the variety of their different services and their readiness to talk about them, gave me a good insight into the inner relationship between the landed aristocracy and their retainers. In recalling these circumstances I thankfully acknowledge how my ever-tender loving destiny took pains kindly to prepare me for each vocation next to come. I had never before had the opportunity to see the

---

* Upper Palatinate, a province in the north of Bavaria.

mode of keeping accounts used on a great estate, to say nothing of keeping them myself, and here I had this very work to do, and that after a plan both ample and clear, in which every particular, down to the single details, was carefully provided for. This was of the greatest service to me. Precisely the conduct of such well-ordered accounts was to be my work later on ; therefore, having the general plan I have referred to firmly established in my mind, and being well practised in its operation, I set off well prepared for my new sphere of work. Thanks to this, I was able to satisfy most completely not only my new employer, but also his lady, who used to examine everything minutely with severe scrutiny.

The surroundings of Herr Von Dewitz's estate were uncommonly pretty for that part of the country. Lakes and hills and the fresh foliage of trees abounded, and what Nature had perhaps overlooked here and there Art had made good. My good fortune has always led me amongst pretty natural scenery. I have ever thankfully enjoyed what Nature has spread before my eyes, and she has always been in true motherly unity with me. As soon as I had gained some facility in it my new work became simple, ran its regular course which was repeated week by week, and gave me time to think about my own improvement.

However, my engagement on this estate was, after all, but a short one. The bent of my life and disposition was already taken. A star had arisen within my mind which I was impelled to follow. On this account I could regard my employment at this time only as a sheet anchor, to be let go as soon as an opportunity offered itself to resume my vocation. This opportunity was not long in making its appearance.

My uncle (Hoffmann), who, like my brother, bore me always lovingly in his thoughts, had lately died. Even on his deathbed he thought of me, and charged my brother to do all he could to find me some settled occupation for life, and at any rate to prevent me from leaving the post I held at the moment before I had some reasonable prospect of a secure and better engagement elsewhere. Providence willed it otherwise. His death, through the small inheritance which thereby came to me, gave me the means of fulfilling the dearest wish of my heart. So wonderfully does God direct the fate of men.

I must mention one circumstance before I part for ever in this account of my life from my gentle, loving second-father. On my journey to Mecklenburg, when I saw my uncle (at Stadt-Ilm) for the last time, I had the deep joy of a talk with him, such as a trusting father might hold with his grown-up son, bound to him by every tie of affection. He freely pointed out the faults which had shown themselves in my boyhood, and told me of the anxiety they had at one time caused him, and in this way he went back to the time when I was taken into his family, and to the causes of that. " I loved your mother very dearly," said he ; " indeed, she was my favourite out of all my brothers and sisters. In you I seemed to see my sister once more, and for her love I took charge of you, and bestowed on you that affection which hitherto had been hers alone." And dear as my own mother had become to me already through the many kind things I had heard said of her, so that I had even formed a distinct conception of what she was like, and seemed actually to remember her, she became even dearer to me after these reminiscences of my uncle than before, for did I not owe to her this noble and high-minded second-father? My conversation with my uncle first made clear to me what in later life I have found repeatedly confirmed—that the sources, springs, or motives of one's present actions often lie far away beyond the present time, outside the present circumstances, and are altogether disconnected with the persons with whom one is concerned at the moment then passing. I have also repeatedly observed in the course of my life that ties are the faster, the more enduring, and the truer the more they spring from higher, universal, and impersonal sources.

The person who in Mecklenburg stood next above me in position in the house and in the family was the private tutor, whom I found already there—a young doctor of philosophy of Göttingen University. We did not come much into contact on the whole, since he as a university graduate took a far higher stand than I ; but through him I came into some connection with the clergymen of the district, and this was of benefit to me. As for the farmers, the bailiffs, etc., their hospitable nature was quite sufficient of itself to afford me a hearty welcome. Thus I lived in a way I had for a long time felt I much needed, amidst many-sided companionable good-fellowship, cheerful and free. Healthy as I was in body and soul, in head and heart, my thoughts full of brightness and cheerfulness, it was not long before my mind again felt an eager desire for higher culture. The young tutor went away, and after his departure my craving for culture grew keener and keener, for I missed the intellectual converse I had been able to hold with him. But I was soon again to receive succour.

The President,* besides the family at home, had two sons at the Pädagogium in Halle.† They came to visit their parents, accompanied by their special tutor, a gentleman destined to become famous later on as the renowned scholar, Dr. Wollweide.

Dr. Wollweide was a mathematician and a physicist, and I found him freely communicative. He was so kind as to mention and explain to me the many various problems he had set before himself to work out. This caused my long slumbering and suppressed love for mathematics as a science, and for physics, to spring up again, fully awake. For some time past my tendency had leaned more and more towards architecture, and, indeed, I had now firmly determined to choose that as my profession, and to study it henceforth with all earnestness. My intellectual cravings and the choice of a profession seemed at last to run together, and I felt continually bright and happy at the thought. I seized the opportunity of the presence of the scholar whom I have named to learn from him what were the best books on those subjects which promised to be useful to me, and my first care was to become possessed of them. Architecture was now vigorously studied, and other books, too, were not suffered to lie idle.

The following books took great hold upon me : Pröschke's "Fragments on Anthropology" (a small unpretending book), Novalis' Works, and Arndt's "Germany" and "Europe." ‡ The

---

* Herr Von Dewitz, his employer.

† The Pädagogium in Halle answered somewhat to our grammar schools with a mixture of boarders and day-scholars. It was founded by Francke in 1712, after the ideas of the famous Basedow, and was endowed by means of a public subscription.

‡ These were two pamphlets by the famous patriot and poet Ernst Moritz Arndt (1769-1860), published in 1805.

first of these at one stroke drew together, so that I could recognise in them myself as a connected whole, my outer existence, my inner character, my disposition, and the course of my life. I for the first time realised myself and my life as a single entity in contrast to the whole world outside of me.* The second book lay before me the most secret emotions, perceptions, and intentions of my inmost soul, clear, open, and vivid. If I parted with that book it seemed as if I had parted with myself; if anything happened to the book I felt as though it had happened to me, only more deeply and with greater pain. The third book taught me of man in his broad historical relations, set before me the general life of my kind as one great whole, and showed me how I was bound to my own nation, both to my ancestors and my contemporaries. Yet the service this last book had done me was hardly recognised at this time; for my thoughts were bent on a definite outward aim, that of becoming an architect. But I could at all events recognise the new eager life which had seized me, and to mark this change to myself, I now began to use as a Christian name the last instead of the first of my baptismal names.† Other circumstances also impelled me to make this change; and, further, it freed me from the memory of the many disagreeable impressions of my boyhood which clustered round the name I was then called.

The time had come when I could no longer remain satisfied with my present occupation; and I therefore sent in my resignation. The immediate outward circumstance which decided me was this. I had kept up a correspondence with the young man whom I had known as a private tutor when I held a Government clerkship in Bamberg, and who left his situation to go to Frankfurt, and then on into France.‡ He had afterwards lived some time in Frankfurt, occupying himself with teaching, and now was again a private tutor in a merchant's house in the Netherlands. I im-

---

* That is, Froebel realised the distinction of the subject-world from the object-world.

† That is, he signed Wilhelm Froebel instead of Friedrich Froebel, for a time. It cannot have been for long, however.

‡ The young man mentioned on page 39.

parted to him my desire to leave my present post, and to seek a situation with an architect; and asked his opinion whether I should not be most likely to effect my object at Frankfurt, where so many streams of diverse life and of men intermingle. And as my friend was accurately acquainted with the ins and outs of Frankfurt life, I asked him to give me such indications as he could of the best road to take towards the fulfilment of my designs. My friend entered heartily into my project, and wrote to me that he intended himself to spend some time in Frankfurt again in the early summer; and he suggested that if I could manage to be there at the same time, a mutual consideration of the whole matter on the spot would be the best way of going to work. In consequence of this I at once firmly decided to leave my situation in the following spring, and to join my friend at Frankfurt. But where was I to find the money necessary for such a journey? I had required the whole of my salary up till now to cover my personal expenses and the settlement of some debts I had run up at Bamberg.

In this perplexity I wrote again to my eldest brother, who had up till now understood me so well, and I asked him for assistance. I was at this time in a peculiar dilemma. On the one hand, I felt very keenly that I must get out of my present position, while on the other, by my unchanging changeableness I feared to wear out the indulgence and patience of my worthy brother. In this strait I just gave him what seemed to me as I wrote it an exact account of my real state of mind; telling him that I could only find my life-aim in a continual striving towards inward perfection.

My brother's answer arrived. With a joyful tremor and agitation I held it in my hands. For hours together I carried it about me before I unsealed it, for days together before I read it; it seemed so improbable that my brother would feel himself able to help me towards the accomplishment of the desire of my soul, and I feared to find in that letter the frustration of my life's endeavour. When, after some days of vacillation between hope and doubt, I could bear the situation no longer, and opened the letter, I was not a little astonished that it began by addressing me at once in terms of the most moving sympathy. As I read on the contents agitated me deeply. The letter gave me the news of my beloved uncle's death, and informed me of legacies left by him to me and my brothers. Thus fate itself, though in a manner so deeply affecting, provided me with the means for working out my next plan.

The die was now cast. From this moment onwards my inner life received a quite new signification and a fresh character, and yet I was unconscious of all this. I was like a tree which flowers and knows it not. My inward and outward vocation and endeavour, my true life-destiny and my apparent life-aim were still, however, in a state of separation, and indeed of conflict, of which I had not the remotest conception. My resolve held firm to make architecture my profession ; it was purely as a future architect that I took leave of all my companions.

At the end of April 1805, with peace in my heart, cheerfulness in my soul, an eager disposition, and a mind full of energy, I quitted my old surroundings. The first days of an unusually lovely May (and I might here again recall what I pointed out above, that my inner and personal life invariably went familiarly hand in hand with external Nature) I spent with a friend, as a holiday, in the best sense of the word. This was a dear friend of mine, who lived on an exceedingly finely-situated farm in the Uckermark.* Art had improved the beauty of the somewhat simple natural features of the place, in the most cunningly-devised fashion. In this beautiful, retired, and even solitary spot, I flitted, as it were, from one flower to another like a very butterfly. I had always passionately loved Nature in her adornments of colour and of dewy pearls, and clung to her closely with the gladsomeness of youth. Here I made the discovery that a land-scape which we look upon in sympathetic mood shines with enhanced brilliancy ; or as I put the truth into words at the time, "The more intimately we attach ourselves to Nature, the more she glows with beauty and returns us all our affection." This was the first time my mind had ventured to give expression

---

* The pretty district bordering the river Ucker, in pleasing contrast with the sandy plains of Brandenburg ; it lies at no great distance from Berlin, so that it forms the favourite goal for a short excursion with the people of that arid city

to a sentiment which thrilled my soul. Often in later life has this phrase proved itself a very truth to me. My friend one day begged me to write something in his album : I did so unwillingly. To write anything borrowed went against me, for it jarred with the relations existing between me and the book's owner ; and to think of anything original was a task I felt to be almost beyond my powers. However, after long thinking it over in the open air, comparing my friend's life and my own in all their aspects, I decided upon the following phrase :—" To thee may destiny soon grant a settled home and a loving wife ! To me, while she drives me restless abroad, may she leave but just so much time as to allow me fairly to discern my relations with my inmost self and with the world." Then my thoughts grew clear, and I continued, " Thou givest man bread ; let my aim be to give man himself."

I did not even then fully apprehend the meaning of what I had said and written, or I could not of course have held so firmly to my architecture scheme. I knew as yet neither myself nor my real life, neither my goal nor my life's path thither. And long afterwards, when I had for some time been engaged upon my true vocation, I was not a little astonished over the prophetic nature of this album-phrase of mine.

In later life I have often observed that a man's spirit, when it first begins to stir within him, utters many a far-away prophetic thought, which yet, in riper age, attains its realisation, its consummation. I have especially noticed this recently in bright-minded and active children ; in fact, I have often been quite astounded at the really deep truths expressed by them in their butterfly life. I seemed to catch glimpses of a symbolic truth in this ; as if indeed the human soul were even already beginning to shake itself free from its chrysalis-wrapping, or were bursting off the last fragments of the eggshell.

In May 1805, while on my journey, I visited my eldest brother, of whom I have so often spoken, and shall have yet so often to speak, and found him in another district, to which he had been appointed minister. He was as kind and full of affection as ever ; and instead of blaming me, spoke with especial approval of my new plans. He told me of projects which had allured him in his

4

youth, and still allured, but which he had lacked the strength of mind
to speak of. His father's advice and authority had overawed him
in youth, and now the chain of a settled position in life held him
fast. To follow the inward voice faithfully and without swerving
was the advice he offered me, and he wrote this memorandum in
my album when I left him, as a life motto :—" The task of man
is a struggle towards an end. Do your duty as a man, dear
brother, with firmness and resolution, fight against the difficulties
which will thrust themselves in your path, and be assured you
will attain the end."

Thus cheered by sympathy and approval, I went my way
from my brother's, strengthened and confirmed in my determination. My road lay over the Wartburg.* Luther's life and
fame were then not nearly so well appreciated and so generally
understood as now, after the Tercentenary festival of the Reformation.† My early education had not been of the kind to give me
a complete survey of Luther's life and its struggle ; I was hardly
thoroughly acquainted indeed with the separate events of it. Yet
I had learnt in some sort to appreciate this fighter for the truth,
by having in my last years at school to read aloud the Augsburg
Confession to the assembled congregation during the afternoon
service on certain specified Sundays, according to an old-fashioned
Church custom.‡ I was filled with a deep sense of reverence as
I climbed " Luther's path," thinking at the same time that Luther
had left much behind still to be done, to be rooted out, or to be
built up.

Shortly before Midsummer Day, as I had arranged with my
friend, I reached Frankfurt. During my many weeks' journey in
th lovely springtime, my thoughts had had time to grow calm
and collected. My friend, too, was true to his word ; and we at
once set to work together to prepare a prosperous future for me.
The plan of seeking a situation with an architect was still firmly

---

* Whither Luther fled for refuge after the Diet of Worms in 1521 ; and
where, protected by the Elector of Saxony, he lay concealed for a year
During this year he translated the New Testament.

† Held all over Protestant Germany in 1817.

‡ Our children still in like manner "say their cateohism" at afternoon
church in old-fashioned country places.

held to, and circumstances seemed favourable for its realisation ; but my friend at last advised me to secure a livelihood by giving lessons for a time, until we should find something more definite than had yet appeared. Every prospect of a speedy fulfilment of my wishes seemed to offer, and yet in proportion as my hopes grew more clear, a certain feeling of oppression manifested itself more and more within me. I soon began seriously to ask myself, therefore :—

"How is this ? Canst thou do work in architecture worthy of a man's life ? Canst thou use it to the culture and the ennoblement of mankind ? "

I answered my own question to my satisfaction. Yet I could not conceal from myself that it would be difficult to follow this profession conformably with the ideal I had now set before me. Notwithstanding this, I still remained faithful to my original scheme, and soon began to study under an architect with a view to fitting myself for my new profession.

My friend, unceasingly working towards the accomplishment of my views, introduced me to a friend of his, Herr Gruner, the headmaster at that time of the Frankfurt Model School,* which had not long been established. Here I found open-minded young people who met me readily and ingenuously, and our conversation soon ranged freely over life and its many-sided aspects. My own life and its object were also brought forward and talked over. I spoke openly, manifesting myself just as I was, saying what I knew and what I did not know about myself.

"Oh," said Gruner, turning to me, "give up architecture ; it is not your vocation at all. Become a teacher. We want a teacher in our own school. Say you agree, and the place shall be yours."

My friend was for accepting Gruner's proposal, and I began to hesitate. Added to this, an external circumstance now came to my knowledge which hastened my decision. I received the news namely, that the whole of my testimonials, and particularly those

---

* This school, still in existence up to 1865 and later, but now no longer in being, had been founded under Gruner, a pupil of Pestalozzi, to embody and carry out the educational principles of the latter.

that I had received in Jena, which were amongst them, had been lost. They had been sent to a gentleman who took a lively interest in my affairs, and I never found out through what mischance they were lost. I now read this to mean that Providence itself had thus broken up the bridge behind me, and cut off all return. I deliberated no longer, but eagerly and joyfully seized the hand held out to me, and quickly became a teacher in the Model School of Frankfurt-on-the-Main.*

The watchword of teaching and of education was at this time the name of PESTALOZZI. It soon became evident to me that Pestalozzi was to be the watchword of my life also; for not only Gruner, but also a second teacher at the school, were pupils of Pestalozzi, and the first-named had even written a book on his method of teaching. The name had a magnetic effect upon me, the more so as during my self-development and self-education it had seemed to me an aspiration—a something perhaps never to be familiarly known, yet distinct enough, and at all events inspiriting. And now I recalled how in my early boyhood, in my father's house, I had got a certain piece of news out of some newspaper or another, or at least that is how the matter stood in my memory. I gathered that in Switzerland a man of forty, who lived retired from the world,—Pestalozzi by name,—had taught himself, alone and unaided, reading, writing, and arithmetic. Just at that time I was feeling the slowness and insufficiency of my own development, and this news quieted me, and filled me with the hope and trust that I, too, might, through my own endeavour, repair the deficiencies of my bringing-up. As I have grown older I have also found it consolatory to remark how the culture of vigorous, capable men has not seldom been acquired remarkably late in life. And in general I must acknowledge it as part of the groundwork under-lying my life and the evolution of my character, that the contemplation of the actual existences of real men always wrought upon my soul, as it were, by a fruitful rain and the genial warmth of sunshine; while the isolated truths these lives enshrined, the

* There is a smaller town called Frankfurt, on the Oder. "Am Main," or 'An der Oder," is, therefore, added to the greater or the smaller Frankfurt respectively, for distinction's sake.

principles those who lived them had thought out and embodied in some phrase or another, fell as precious seed-corn, as it were, or as solvent salt crystals upon my thirsty spirit. And while on this head I cannot help especially calling to mind how deep and lasting was the impression made upon me in my last year at school by the accounts in the Holy Scriptures of the lives of earnestly striving youths and men. I mention it here, but I shall have to return to the subject later on.*

Now to return to the new life which I had begun. It was only to be expected that each thing and all things I heard of Pestalozzi seized powerfully upon me ; and this more especially applies to a sketchy narrative of his life, his aims, and his struggles, which I found in a literary newspaper, where also was stated Pestalozzi's well-known desire and endeavour—namely, in some nook or corner of the world, no matter where, to build up an institution for the education of the poor, after his own heart. This narrative, especially the last point of it, was to my heart like oil poured on fire. There and then the resolution was taken to go and look upon this man who could so think and so endeavour to act, and to study his life and its work.

Three days afterwards (it was towards the end of August 1805) I was already on the road to Yverdon,† where Pestalozzi had not long before established himself. Once arrived there, and having met with the friendliest reception by Pestalozzi and his teachers, because of my introductions from Gruner and his colleagues, I was taken, like every other visitor, to the class-rooms, and there left more or less to my own devices. I was still very inexperienced, both in the theory and practice of teaching, relying chiefly in such things upon my memory of my own school-time, and I was therefore very little fitted for a rigorous examination into details of method and into the way they were connected to form a whole system. The latter point, indeed, was neither clearly thought out, nor was it worked out in practice. What I saw was to me at once elevating and depressing, arousing and also bewil-

---

* He never does, for this interesting record remains a fragment.

† Situate at the head of the lake of Neuchatel, but in the canton of Vaud, in Switzerland.

dering. My visit lasted only a fortnight. I worked away and tried to take in as much as I could ; especially as, to help me in the duties I had undertaken, I felt impelled to give a faithful account in writing of my views on the whole system, and the effect it had produced upon me. With this idea I tried to hold fast in my memory all I heard. Nevertheless I soon felt that heart and mind would alike come to grief in a man of my disposition if I were to stay longer with Pestalozzi, much as I desired to do so. At that time the life there was especially vigorous ; internally and externally it was a living, moving, stirring existence, for Prince Hardenberg, commissioned by the Austrian Government, had come to examine thoroughly into Pestalozzi's work.*

The fruits of my short stay with Pestalozzi were as follows :—

In the first place, I saw the whole training of a great educational institution, worked upon a clear and firmly-settled plan of teaching. I still possess the "teaching-plan" of Pestalozzi's institution in use at that time. This teaching-plan contains, in my opinion, much that is excellent, somewhat also that is prejudicial. Excellent, I thought, was the contrivance of the so-called "exchange classes." † In each subject the instruction was always given through the entire establishment at the same time. Thus the subjects for teaching were settled for every class, but the pupils were distributed amongst the various classes according to their proficiency in the subject in hand, so that the whole body of pupils was redistributed in quite a distinct division for each subject. The advantage of this contrivance struck me as so undeniable and so forcible that I have never since relinquished it in my educational work, nor could I now bring myself to do so. The prejudicial side of the teaching-plan, against which I intuitively rebelled, although my own tendencies on the subject were as yet so vague and dim, lay, in my opinion, in its incompleteness and its onesidedness. Several subjects of teaching

---

* Austria was not the only country alive to tne importance of this new teaching. Prussia and Holland also sent commissioners to study Pestalozzi's system, and so did many other smaller states. The Czar (Alexander I.) sent for Pestalozzi to a personal interview at Basel.

† *Wandernde Classen.* Some of our later English schools have adopted a similar plan.

and education highly important to the all-round harmonious development of a man seemed to me thrust far too much into the background, treated in step-motherly fashion, and superficially worked out.

The results of the arithmetical teaching astounded me, yet I could not follow it into its larger applications and wider extent. The mechanical rules of this branch of instruction seemed to whirl me round and round as in a whirlpool. The teacher was Krüsi. The teaching, in spite of the brilliant results within its own circle, and in spite of the sharpness of the quickened powers of perception and comprehension in the children by which it attained those results, yet, to my personal taste, had something too positive in its setting forth, too mechanical in its reception. And Josias Schmid * had already, even at that time, felt the imperfection of this branch of instruction. He imparted to me the first ground-principles of his later work on the subject, and his ideas at once commanded my approval, for I saw they possessed two important properties, manysidedness and an exhaustive scientific basis.

The teaching of drawing was also very incomplete, especially in its first commencement ; but drawing from right-angled prisms with equal sides, in various lengths, which was one of the exercises required at a later stage, and drawing other mathematical figures by means of which the comprehension of the forms of actual objects of every-day life might be facilitated were much more to my mind. Schmid's method of drawing had not yet appeared.

In physical geography, the usual school course, with its many-coloured maps, had been left far behind. Tobler, an active young man, was the principal teacher in this section. Still, even this branch had far too much positive instruction † for me. Particularly unpleasant to me was the commencement of the course, which began with an account of the bottom of the sea, although

---

* One of Pestalozzi's teachers, to whom especially was confided the arrangement of the arithmetical studies.

† By positive instruction Froebel means learning by heart, or by being told results ; as distinguished from actual education or development of the faculties, and the working out of results by pupils for themselves.

the pupils could have no conception of their own as to its nature or dimensions. Nevertheless the teaching aroused astonishment, and carried one involuntarily along with it through the impression made by the lightning-quickness of the answers of the children.

In natural history I heard only the botany. The principal teacher, who had also prepared the plan of instruction in this subject for all the school, was Hopf, like the rest an active young man. The school course arranged and carried out by him had much that was excellent. In each separate instance—for example, the shape and position of leaves, flowers, etc.—he would first obtain all the possible varieties of form by question and answer between the class and himself, and then he would select from the results the form which was before them in nature. These lessons, which were in this way made so attractive, and whose merits spoke for themselves, showed, however, when it came to practical application, an unpractical, I had almost said, a self-contradictory aspect.

(When, afterwards, in 1808, I visited Yverdon for the second time, I found to my regret neither Tobler nor Hopf there.)

With the method used for the German language I could not at all bring myself into sympathy, although it has been introduced into later school books elsewhere. Here also the arbitrary and non-productive style of teaching ran strongly counter to me at every step.

Singing was taught from figures.* Reading was taught from Pestalozzi's well-known " A. B. C."

[Memorandum.—All this lay dark within me, its value unrecognised even by myself. But my intellectual position tended to become more settled by passing through these experiences. As to my state at the time, I have, as accurately as may be, described it above, as at once exalted and depressed, animated and dull. That Pestalozzi himself was carried away and

---

* This must mean the system invented by Rousseau, a modern development of which is the Chevé system now widely used on the Continent. In England the tonic-sol-fa notation, which uses syllables instead of figures, but which rests fundamentally on the same principles, is much more familiar.

bewildered by this great intellectual machine of his appears from the fact that he could never give any definite account of his idea, his plan, his intention. He always said, "Go and see for yourself" (very good for him who knew *how* to look, how to hear, how to perceive); "it works splendidly!" * It was at that time, indeed, surprising and inexplicable to me that Pestalozzi's loving character did not win every one's heart as it won mine, and compel the staff of teachers to draw together into a connected whole, penetrated with life and intellectual strength in every part. His morning and evening addresses were deeply touching in their simplicity; and yet I remarked in them even already at that time some slight traces of the unhappy dissensions afterwards to arise. †]

I left Yverdon in mid-October (1805) with a settled resolution to return thither as soon as possible for a longer stay. As soon as I got back to Frankfurt, I received my definite appointment from the Consistorium.‡ The work that awaited me upon my arrival from Switzerland at the Model School (which was, in fact, properly two schools, one for boys and one for girls) was a share in the arrangement of an entirely new educational course and teaching-plan for the whole establishment. The school contained four or five classes of boys and two or three of girls; altogether about two hundred children. The staff consisted of four permanent masters and nine visiting masters.

As I threw myself heartily into the consideration of the necessities and the present position of the school, and of the instruction given there, the working out of this plan was left almost wholly in my hands, under the conditions imposed upon us. The scheme I produced not only succeeded in winning the approbation of the authorities, but proved itself during a long period

---

* "*Geht und schaut, es geht ungehür (ungeheuer).*"

† The miserable quarrels between Niederer and Schmid, which so distressed the later years of Pestalozzi, are here referred to.

‡ A Consistorium in Germany is a sort of clerical council or convocation, made up of the whole of the Established clergy of a province, and supervising Church and school matters throughout that province, under the control of the Ministry of Religion and Education. No educator could establish a school or take a post in a school without the approval of this body.

of service beneficial in the highest degree, both to the institution itself and to its efficiency; notwithstanding that it put the teachers to some considerable personal inconvenience, as well as making larger claims upon their time than was usual.

The subjects of instruction which fell to my share were arithmetic, drawing, physical geography, and German. I generally taught in the middle classes. In a letter to my brother I spoke of the impression made upon me by my first lesson to a class of thirty or forty boys ranging from nine to eleven; it seemed as if I had found something I had never known, but always longed for, always missed, as if my life had at last discovered its native element. I felt as happy as the fish in the water, the bird in the air.

But before I pursue this side of the development of my life I must touch upon another which was far more important to the evolution of my character as man, as teacher, and as educationist, and which, indeed, soon absorbed the first within itself.

Not long after my old friend, to meet with whom I had come to Frankfurt, had introduced me to Gruner, he went back himself to his work as private tutor. Afterwards he heard of a family (in Frankfurt) desiring a private tutor for the sons. Since he could not introduce me personally to this family he did so by letter, and several weeks before my journey to Yverdon he had, in fact, written to them about me in very kindly terms. It was for three sons principally that instruction and education were required. They came to see me, and after they had gone their personal peculiarities and their previous teaching and training, with the results, were fully described to me, and I was then consulted as to their future education. Now to education as an object * I had in truth never yet given a thought, and the question threw me into great perplexity. Nevertheless it required an answer, and moreover a precise answer.

In the life and circumstances of these lads I discovered frequent similarities with my own boyhood, which sprang to my memory as I listened. I could therefore answer the questions which were

---

* That is, the education of other minds than his own; something beyond mere school-teaching.

put to me out of the development and educational experiences of my own life ; and my reply, torn as it was from actual life, keenly felt and vigorously expressed, bore upon it the stamp of truth. It was satisfactory to the parents ; and education—development, which hitherto had been subjective alone for me—that is, as self-development—now took an objective form, a change which was distinctly painful to me. Long, long it was before I could bring this business of education into a form expressible by words. I only knew education, and I could only educate, through direct personal association. This, then, I cultivated to the best of my power, following the path whither my vocation and my life now called me.

To say truth, I had a silent inward reluctance towards private tutorship. I felt the constant interruptions and the piece-meal nature of the work inseparable from the conditions of the case, and hence I suspected that it might want vitality ; but the trusting indulgence with which I was met, and especially the clear, bright, friendly glance which greeted me from the two younger lads, decided me to undertake to give the boys lessons for two hours a day, and to share their walks. The actual teaching was to be in arithmetic and German. The first was soon arranged. I simply followed Pestalozzi's course. But as to the language I encountered great difficulties. I began by teaching it from the regular school-books then used, and indeed still in use. I prepared myself to the best of my ability for each lesson, and worked up whatever I felt myself ignorant of in the most careful and diligent way. But the mode of teaching employed in these books frustrated my efforts. I could neither get on myself nor get my pupils on with it. So I began to take for my method Pestalozzi's "Mothers' Book." In this way we went on much better, but still I was not satisfied ; and, indeed, I may say that for a very long time no system of instruction in German did satisfy me.

In arithmetic, by using the "Tables of Units "* in Pestalozzi's

---

* *Einertabelle;* tables or formulas extending to units only ; a system embodied to a large extent in Sonnenschein's "ABC of Arithmetic," for teaching just the first elements of the art.

pamphlet, I arrived at the same results which I had seen in Switzerland. Very often my pupils had the answer ready when the last word of the question had scarcely been spoken. Yet I presently found out some defects in this method of teaching, of which I shall speak later on.*

When we were out walking together, I endeavoured to my utmost to penetrate into the lives of the children, and so to influence them for good. I lived my own early life over again, but in a happier way, for it now lay clear and intelligible before me in its special as well as its general characteristics.

All my thoughts and work were now directed to the subject of the culture and education of man. This period of my life became full of zeal, of active development, of advancing culture, and, in consequence, of happiness. And my life in the Model School also, with my boys and with my excellent colleagues, unusually clever men, was very elevating and encouraging.

Owing to the position and surroundings of the school buildings, which, though not apparently extensive as seen from the street, contained a considerable courtyard and a spacious garden, the scholars enjoyed perfect freedom of exercise, and could play just as they liked in courtyard or garden ; with the result, moreover, of thereby affording a most important opportunity to the various teachers of becoming really intimate with the characters of the boys they taught. And there grew up out of all this a voluntary resolution on the part of the teachers that every teacher should take his boys for a walk once a week. Each adopted the method he liked best ; some preferred to occupy the time of the walk over a permanent subject; others preferred leaving the subject to chance. I usually occupied my class with botanising ; and also as geographical master, I turned these occasions to profit by leading on my boys to think for themselves and to apprehend the relations of various parts of the earth's surface : on these and other perceptions gained in this way I based my instruction in physiography, making them my point of departure.

The town was at once my starting-place and my centre. From

---

* Like other matters, this, too, has been left undone, as far as the present (unfinished) letter is concerned.

it I extended our observations to the right and to the left, on this side and on that. I took the river Main as a base line, just as it lay ; or I used the line of hills or the distant mountains. I settled firmly the direction of the four quarters of the compass. In everything I followed the leading of Nature herself, and with the data so obtained I worked out a representation of the place from direct observation, and on a reduced scale, in some level spot of ground or sandy tract carefully chosen for the purpose. When my representation (or map) was thoroughly understood and well impressed on every one's mind, then we reconstructed it in school on a black board placed horizontally. The map was first sketched by teachers and pupils between them, and then each pupil had to do it by himself as an exercise. These representations of the earth's surface of ours had a round contour, resembling the circular outline of the visible horizon.

At the next public examination of the school, I was fortunate enough, although this first attempt was full of imperfections, to win the unanimous approval of the parents present ; and not only that, but the especial commendation of my superiors. Every one said, "That is how physiography* should be taught. A boy must first learn all about his home before he goes further afield." My boys were as well acquainted with the surroundings of the town as with their own rooms at home ; and gave rapid and striking answers as to all the natural peculiarities of the neighbourhood. This course was the fountain-head of the teaching method which I afterwards thoroughly worked out, and which has now been in use for many years.

In arithmetic I did not take the lower, but the middle classes ; and here also my teaching received cheering encomiums.

In drawing I also taught the middle classes. My method in this subject was to work at the thorough comprehension and the representation of planes and solids in outline, rising from the simplest forms to complex combinations. I not only had the gratification of obtaining good results, which thoroughly satisfied those who tested them, but also of seeing my pupils work with pleasure, with ardour, and with individuality.

---

* *Erdkunde.*

In the girls' school I had to teach orthography* in one of the elementary classes. This lesson, ordinarily standing by itself, disconnected with anything, I based upon correct pronunciation.† The teaching was imperfect, certainly ; but it nevertheless gained an unmistakable charm for both teacher and pupils ; and, finally, its results were very satisfactory.

In one of the other classes of the girls' school I taught preparatory drawing. I took this by combinations of single lines; but the method was wanting in a logically necessary connection, so that it did not satisfy me. I cannot remember whether the results of this teaching were brought to the test or not.

Such was the outcome of my first attempts as a teacher. The kind indulgence and approval granted to me, more because of my good intentions and the fire of my zeal than for my actual performance, spurred me on to plunge deeper into the inquiry as to the nature of true teaching. But the whole system of a large school must have its settled form, with its previously-appointed teaching-course arranged as to times and subjects; and everything must fit in like a piece of clockwork. My system, on the other hand, called only for ready senses and awakened intellect. Set forms could only tolerate this view of education so far as it served to enliven and quicken them. But I have unfortunately again and again observed during my career, that even the most active life, if its activity and its vitality be not properly understood and urged ever onward, easily stiffens into bony rigidity. Enough, my mind, now fully awakened, could not suffer these set forms, necessary though they were ; and I felt that I must seek out some position in which my nature could unfold itself freely according to the needs of the development of my life and of my mind.

This longing endeavour of life and mind, which could not submit to the fetters of external limitations, may have been the more exaggerated at the time by my becoming acquainted with Arndt's " Fragments on Human Culture,"‡ which I had purchased. This book satisfied at once my character, my resolves, and my

---

* *Recht schreiben.*   † *Recht sprechen.*
‡ One of Arndt's pamphlets, then quite new.

aspirations; and what hitherto lay isolated within me was brought into ordered connection through its pages, while ideas which possessed me without my perceiving them took definite form and expression as the book brought them to light. Indeed, I thought then that Arndt's book was the bible of education.

In those days I spoke of my life and my aims in the following words : " I desire to educate men whose feet shall stand on God's earth, rooted fast in Nature, while their head towers up to heaven, and reads its secrets with steady gaze, whose heart shall embrace both earth and heaven, shall enjoy the life of earth and nature with all its wealth of forms, and at the same time shall recognise the purity and peace of heaven, that unites in its love God's earth with God's heaven." In these phrases I now see my former life and aims vividly brought before me as in a picture.

Little by little a desire gained strength within me to free myself from my engagement at the Model School, to which I had bound myself as teacher for at least three years. The headmaster (Gruner), whom I have already named, was sufficiently a student of men to have perceived that so excitable a man as I could never work harmoniously in such an institution as that which he directed; so I was released from my engagement, under the condition that I should provide a suitable successor. Fate was propitious to me once more. I found a young private tutor with whom I had long been in friendly correspondence, and who had all those qualities which were lacking in me. He was not only thoroughly proficient in the grammar of his mother tongue (German), but also in the grammar of the classical tongues; and, if I am not mistaken, in French also. He had a knowledge of geography far beyond anything I could boast, was acquainted with history, knew arithmetic, possessed some familiarity with botany, —much greater, indeed, than I suspected. . And what was worth more than all this, he was full of vigour in mind, heart, and life. Therefore the school was every way the gainer by my departure, so greatly the gainer indeed, that from that time no further change has been necessary. That same teacher still lives and works in that same post.*

* 1827.

Before I begin a new chapter of my career, there are yet a few things which need mention.

To know French was at that time the order of the day, and not to know it stamped a man at once as of a very low degree of culture. To acquire a knowledge of French, therefore, became one of my chief aims at the moment. It was my good fortune to obtain instruction from an unrivalled teacher of French, M. Perrault, a Frenchman by birth, who still, even though an old man, diligently worked at the study of his mother tongue, and who at the same time wrote and spoke German with elegance. I pursued the study with ardour, taking two lessons a day, because I desired to reach a certain proficiency by a given time. Slow, however, were my steps, for I was far from having a sufficient knowledge of my own tongue whereon to build a bridge that might carry me into French. I never could properly acquire what I did not fully understand in such a way that it had a living meaning for me; and so from all the genuine zeal and considerable cost which I spent over this study I gained by no means a corresponding result; but I did learn a good deal, much more even than I then knew how to turn to account. My teacher cast on one side all the usual grammatical difficulties of French study, he aimed at imparting the language as a living thing. But I with my ignorance of language could not completely follow this free method of teaching; and yet, nevertheless, I felt that the teacher had fully grasped the meaning and the method of his work, and I always enjoyed the lessons on this account. He was especially successful in accustoming my ear to the French pronunciation, always separating and reducing it to its simple sounds and tones, and never merely saying " this is pronounced like the German *p*, or *b*, or *ä*, or *ŏ*," etc. The best thing resulting from this course of study was the complete exposure of my ignorance of German grammar. I must do myself the justice to say that I had given myself extraordinary trouble over the works of the most celebrated German grammarians, trying to bring life and interconnection or even a logical consequence into German grammar; but I only confused myself the worse thereby. One man said one thing, another quite the reverse; and not one of all of them, as far as I could see, had educed his theories from the life and nature of the speech itself. I turned away a second time, quite disheartened, from the German grammarians, and once more took my own road. But unfortunately the dry forms of grammar had, quite against my own will, stuck like scales over my eyes, dimming my perceptions; I could find no means to rid myself of them, and they wrought fatally upon me now and long afterwards. The more thoroughly I knew them the more they stiffened and crushed me.

My departure from the school was now arranged, and I could let my mind pursue its development free and unshackled. As heretofore, so now also, my kindly fate came lovingly to my help : I can never speak of it with sufficient thankfulness. The three lads to whom I had hitherto given private instruction in arithmetic and language now needed a tutor, as their former tutor was leaving them. The confidential charge was laid upon me, because I of all men best knew their nature and its needs, ι f seeking out some fit teacher and educator for them from aι ιongst my acquaintance. As for myself this tutor business lay far from my own thoughts, and I therefore looked round me in every direction, and with all earnestness, for some one else. Amongst others I applied to my eldest brother, telling him my views as to the necessary requirements of a true educator.

My brother wrote back very decidedly and simply, that he could not propose any one to me as a teacher and educator who would fulfil the requirements I had set forth, and further, he did not think I should ever be able to find such a person ; for if one should be found possessing ample knowledge and experience of life in its external aspects, he would be deficient in a vigorous inner life of his own, and in the power to recognise and foster it in himself and his pupils ; and, on the other hand, another man who might have this power would be deficient in the first-named (practical) qualities. I reported the result of my labours. It caused much disappointment, indeed it could not be otherwise, because the welfare of the children was really sought, in all love and truth, and the highest and best obtainable at that day was desired on their behalf. The family did not venture to press the post upon me personally, knowing my love of freedom and independence.

So stood matters for several months. At last, moved by my

5

earnest affection for the lads, and by my care to deserve the confidence with which their mother had entrusted to my hands the provision for their education, I endeavoured to look at things from the point of view of their parents. ˙ This brought me at last to the determination to become myself the educator and teacher of the lads. After a hard struggle with myself, the hardest and most exhausting I had undergone for a long time, I made known my decision. It was thankfully received, and understood quite in the spirit which had actuated me in forming it.

I communicated my decision to Gruner, with whom I still kept in the friendliest relation. He looked at me with downright astonishment, and said, " You will lose all hopes of the position you have so long sought and waited for." I replied that I should protect myself as to my position and my relations with others by a very definite written contract. To which the man of experience retorted, " Certainly, and everything will be punctually fulfilled, so that you cannot say that any one condition of all those you stood out so firmly for has failed to be observed ; nevertheless you will find you will lose on all points." So spake experienced shrewdness, and what had I to set against it ? I spoke of the educational necessities and wants of these children. "Good," said he, " then you will leave your own educational necessities and your own wants out of the question ? " How it mortified me, that worldly wisdom should be able to speak thus, and that I was unable to controvert it ! We talked no more about the matter.

And keen as was the internal conflict over this decision and this resolve of mine, equally keen was the external contest which I had to wage in entering on my new post.

There were, namely, two immutable conditions in our agreement. One was that I should never be compelled to live in town with my pupils, and that when I began my duties my pupils should be handed over entirely to my care, without any restriction ; that they should follow me into the country, and there form a restricted and perfectly isolated circle, and that when they returned to town life my duties as preceptor should be at an end. The time for beginning my new career drew nigh. As the stipulated dwelling for myself and my pupils was not yet ready,

I was expected to take up my abode, for a few days, with my pupils in their town house. But I felt that it was clear that the least want of firmness at the outset would endanger my whole educational plan ; therefore, I stood firm, and indeed gained my point, though at the price of being called headstrong, self-willed, and stubborn. That my assumption of my post was attended with a sharp contest was a very good and wholesome discipline for me. It was the fitting inauguration of a position and a sphere of work which was henceforth to be attended, for me, with perpetual and never-ending strife.

But as to this family and all its members, my earnest unbending maintenance of my resolve had a most wholesome effect upon them, even to winning in the end their comprehension and approval, though this was later and long after I had quitted the situation. It was ten or eleven years afterwards—that is, four or five years after my departure—that the mother of these lads expressed her entire approval of the adamantine perseverance I had exhibited in my convictions.

I entered my new sphere of educational work in July 1807. I was twenty-five years old, as far as years went, but younger by several years in regard to the development of my character. I neither felt myself so old as I was, nor indeed had I any conception or realisation of my age. I was only conscious of the strength and striving of my life, the extent of my mental culture, the circumstances of my experience in the world, and especially of—what shall I call it ?—the shiftlessness and undeveloped state of my culture as far as its helplessness with the external world was concerned, of my ignorance of life both as to what it really was, and how it showed in its outer aspect. The state of my culture was such as only to serve to plunge me into conflict, through the contradiction and opposition in which I found myself henceforward with all existing methods ; and consequently the whole period of my tutorial career was one continual contest.

It was a salutary thing for me that this was my appointed lot from the very beginning. Now and later on I was therefore able to say to myself by way of consolation and encouragement : " You knew beforehand just how it would be." Still, unpleasantness seldom arrives in exactly the manner expected, and the unex-

pected is always the hardest to bear. Thus it was with me in
this case ; my situation seemed to contain insurmountable difficulties.   I sought the basis for them in imperfect culture ; and the
cause of the disconnected nature of the culture I had been able to
attain, lay, so I perceived, in the interruptions which marred my
university career.   Educator and teacher, however, I had determined to become and to remain ; and as far as I could know
my own feelings and my own powers, I must and would work
out my profession in an independent free fashion of my own,
founded on the view of man and his nature and relationships
which had now begun to dawn upon me.   Yet every man finds it
above all things difficult to understand himself, and especially
hard was it in my own case.   I began to think that I must look
for help outside myself, and seek to acquire from others the
knowledge and experience I needed.

And thus there came to me once again the idea of fitting myself
by continuing my university studies to become founder, principal,
and manager of an educational establishment of my own.   But
the fact was to be considered that I had turned away from the
educational path on which I had entered.   Now, when the imperfection of my training pressed itself upon me, I not only sought
help from Nature as of old, that school allotted to me by fate, but
I turned also for assistance to my fellow-men who had divided
out the whole field of education and teaching into separate departments of science, and had added to these the assistance of a rich
literature.   This need of help so troubled and oppressed me, and
threw my whole nature into such confusion, that I resolved, as
soon as might be, once more to proceed to one of the universities,
and necessarily, therefore, to relinquish as speedily as possible
my occupation as an educator.

As I always discussed everything important with my brother,
I wrote to him on this occasion as usual, telling him of my plans and
of my resolve.   But for this time, at least, my nature was able
to work out its difficulty without his help.   I soon came to see
that I had failed to appreciate my position, and had misunderstood myself ; and, therefore, before I had time to get an answer
from my brother to my first letter I wrote to him again, telling
him that my university plans had been given up, and that my

fixed resolve now was to remain at my post. He rejoiced doubly at my decision, because this time he would have been unable to agree with me.*

No sooner had I firmly come to my decision than I began to apply my thoughts vigorously to the subjects of education and instruction. The first thing that absorbed me was the clear conviction that to educate properly one must share the life of one's pupil. Then came the questions, "What is elementary education? and of what value are the educational methods advocated by Pestalozzi? Above all, what is the purpose of education?"

In answering the question, "What is the purpose of education?" I relied at that time upon the following observations: Man lives in a world of objects, which influence him, and which he desires to influence; therefore he ought to know these objects in their nature, in their conditions, and in their relations with each other and with mankind. Objects have form measurement, and number.

By the expression, "the external world," at this time I meant only Nature; my life was so bound up in natural objects that I altogether passed by the productions of man's art or manufacture. Therefore for a long time it was an effort to me to regard man's handiwork, with Pestalozzi's scholars, Tobler and Hopf, as a proper subject for elementary culture, and it broadened my inward and outward glance considerably when I was able to look upon the world of the works of man as also part of the "external world." In this way I sought, to the extent of such powers as I consciously possessed at that time, to make clear the meaning of all things through man, his relations with himself, and with the external world.

The most pregnant thought which arose in me at this period was this: All is unity, all rests in unity, all springs from unity, strives for and leads up to unity, and returns to unity at last. This striving in unity and after unity is the cause of the several aspects of human life. But between my inner vision and my outer perception, presentation, and action was a great gulf fixed.

---

* He would have refused to countenance Froebel's throwing up his engagement.

Therefore it seemed to me that everything which should or could
be required for human education and instruction must be
necessarily conditioned and given, by virtue of the very nature
of the necessary course of his development, in man's own being,
and in the relationships amidst which he is set. A man, it
seemed to me, would be well educated, when he had been trained
to care for these relationships and to acknowledge them, to master
them and to survey them.

I worked hard, severely hard, during this period, but both the
methods and the aims of education came before me in such an
incoherent heap, so split up into little fragments, and so entirely
without any kind of order, that during several years I did not
make much progress towards my constant purpose of bringing
all educational methods into an orderly sequence and a living
unity. As my habitual and therefore characteristic expression
of my desires then ran, I longed to see, to know, and to show
forth, all things in inter-connection.

For my good fortune, however, there came out about that time
certain educational writings by Seiler,* Jean Paul,† and others.
They supported and elevated me, sometimes by their concurrence
with my own views, expressed above, sometimes by the very
contrary.

The Pestalozzian method I knew, it is true, in its main
principles, but not as a living force, satisfying the needs of man.
What especially lay heavy upon me at this time, however, painfully felt by myself though not apparent to my pupils, was the
utter absence of any organised connection between the subjects
of education. Joyful and unfettered work springs from the conception of all things as one whole, and forms a life and a lifework

---

* Georg Friedrich Seiler (1733-1807), a Bavarian by birth, became a highly-
esteemed clergyman in Coburg. He wrote on religious and moral subjects,
and those amongst the list of his works, the most likely to be alluded to by
Froebel, are "A Bible for Teachers," "Methods of Religious Teaching for
Schools," "Religious Culture for the Young," etc.

† Jean Paul Friedrich Richter (1763-1825). No doubt the celebrated
"Levana," Richter's educational masterpiece, which was published in this
same year, 1807, is here alluded to.

in harmony with the constitution of the universe and resting firmly upon it.

That this was the true education I soon felt fervently convinced, and so my first educational work consisted merely in being with my pupils and influencing them by the power of my life and work; more than this I was not at all in a position to give.

Oh, why is it that man knows so ill and prizes so little the blessings that he possesses for the first time?

When I now seek to make myself clear as to the proper life and work of an educator, my notes of that time rise fresh and fair to meet me. I look back from now into that childhood of my teacher's life, and learn from it; just as I look back into the childhood of my man's life, and survey that, and learn from that, too. Why is all childhood and youth so full of wealth and so unconscious of it, and why does it lose it without knowing it only to learn what it possessed when it is for ever lost? Ought this always to be so? Ought it to be so for every child, for every youth? Will not a time come at last, come perhaps soon, when the experience, the insight, the knowledge of age, and wisdom herself, shall build up a defence, a shelter, a protection for the childhood of youth? Of what use to mankind is the old man's experience and the greybeard's wisdom when they sink into the grave with their possessors?

At first my life and my work with my pupils was confined within narrow limits. It consisted in merely living, lounging, and strolling in the open air, and going for walks. Although I was disgusted with the methods of town education, I did not yet venture to convert life amidst Nature into an educational course. That was taught me by my young pupils themselves; and as from the circumstances of my own culture I eagerly fostered to my utmost every budding sense for Nature that showed itself, there soon developed amongst them a life-encompassing, life-giving, and life-raising enjoyment of natural objects. In the following year * this way of life was further enhanced by the father giving his sons a piece of meadowland for a garden, at the cultivation of which we

---

* 1808.

accordingly worked in common. The greatest delight of my pupils was to make little presents of the produce of their garden to their parents and also to me. How their eyes would gleam with pleasure when they were fortunate enough to be able to accomplish this. Pretty plants and little shrubs from the fields, the great garden of God, were transplanted by us to the children's gardens, and there carefully tended. Great was the joy, especially of the two younger ones, when such a colonist frankly enrolled himself amongst the citizens of the state. From this time forth my own childhood no longer seemed wasted. I acknowledged how entirely different a thing is the cultivation of plants, to one who has watched them and studied them in all the stages of their own free development, from what it is to one who has always stood aloof from Nature.

And here already, living cheerfully and joyfully in the bosom of Nature with my first pupils, I began to tell myself that the training of natural life was closely akin to the training of human life. For did not those gifts of flowers and plants express appreciation and acknowledgment of the love of parents and teacher? Were they not the outcome of the characteristic lovingness and the enthusiastic thankfulness of childhood? A child that of its own accord and of its own free will seeks out flowers, cares for them, and protects them, so that in due time he can weave a garland or make a nosegay with them for his parents or his teacher, can never become a bad child, a wicked man. Such a child can easily be led towards love, towards thankfulness, towards recognition of the fatherliness of God, who gives him these gifts and permits them to grow that he, as a cheerful giver in his turn, may gladden with them the hearts of his parents.

That time of conflict contained within it an element of special and peculiar meaning to myself. It brought before me my past life in its many various stages of development; and especially the chief events which had formed and influenced it, with their causes and their effects. And it always seemed to me of particular importance to go back upon the very earliest occurrences in my life. But of the actual matters of fact of my earliest years very few traces now remained; for my mother, who could have kept them in her memory for me, and from whom I could now have learnt them, had died even before my life had really awakened. Amongst the few relics remaining to me was a written address from my godmother (the so-called Baptismal Letter), which she had sent me immediately after my baptism, according to the Thuringian custom of the time, as a sort of portion or dowry for my entrance into life. It had come into my possession after the death of my father. This letter, of a simple, Christian, tenderly religious, womanly soul, expressed in plain and affecting terms the true relation of the young Christian to that to which by his baptism he had become bound. Through these words the inner life of both mind and soul, of my boyhood and of my youth, was brought before me with all its peace and blessedness; and I could not help seeing how much that I then longed for had since come to pass. My soul, upon this thought, regained that original inspiriting, enlightening, and quickening unity of which I stood so much in need. But at the same time all the resolutions of my boyhood and youth also rushed back upon me, and made it manifest how much more had yet to happen before they, too, were accomplished; and with them they brought the memory of those types and ideals with which the feeble boyish imagination had sought to strengthen itself. But my life had been far too much an inward and strictly personal life to have been able, or even to have dared to stand forth in any outwardly definite form, or to take any fixed relation to other lives, except in matters of feeling and intelligence. Indeed the power of manifesting myself properly was a very late accomplishment with me, and was, in fact, not gained until long after the recommencement of my present educational work.* I cannot now remember, during all the time of this educational work, that my personal life stood out in any way from the usual ordinary existence of men; but before I can speak with certainty upon this point I must procure information as to the circumstances of my earlier life. This much is clear, that my life at the time I am speaking of has remained in my memory only in its general ordinary human aspect. It is true, however, that then, as always

---

* This is in 1827. But the expression of his thought remained a difficult matter with Froebel to the end of his life, a drawback to which many of his friends have borne witness; for instance, Madame von Marenholtz-Bülow.

in my later life, it was and ever has been very difficult to me to separate in thought my inner life from my outer, and to give definite form and outward expression to the inner life, especially as to religious matters.

I dare not deny, that although the definite religious forms of the Church reached my heart readily both by way of the emotions and by sincere conviction, and cleansed and quickened me, yet I have always felt great reluctance to speak of these definite religious forms with others, particularly with pupils and students. I could never make them so clear and living to a simple healthy soul as they were to myself. From this I conclude that the naturally trained child requires no definite Church forms, because the lovingly-fostered, and therefore continuously and powerfully-developed human life, as well as the untroubled child-life also, is and must be in itself a Christian life. I further conclude that a child to whom the deeper truths of life or of religion were given in the dogmatic positive forms of Church creeds would imperatively need when a young man to be surrounded by pure and manly lives, whereby those rigid creeds might be illuminated and quickened into life. Otherwise the child runs great danger of casting away his whole higher life along with the dogmatic religious forms which he has been unable to assimilate. There, indeed, is the most elevated faith to be found, where form and life work towards a whole, shed light upon each other, and go side by side in a sisterly concord, like the inward life with the outward life, or the special with the universal.

But I must return from this long digression, and resume the account of my life and work as an educator.

Bodily exercises were as yet unknown to me in their educational capacity. I was acquainted only with jumping over a cord and with walking on stilts through my own boyish practice therein. As they fell into no relation with our common life, neither with the pursuits and thoughts of my pupils nor with my own, we regarded them purely as childish games.

What the year brings to a man in the season when Nature lies clear and open before him, that it does not bring to him in the season when Nature is more often locked away from his gaze. An l as the two seasons bring diverse gifts, so do they require diverse things in return. In the latter part of the year, when man is perforce driven more upon himself, his occupations should take on more narrowly personal characteristics. Just as the winter's life with nature is more fixed and narrowed, so also is the winter's life with men ; therefore, a boy's life at this time needs material of some definite fashion, or needs fashionless material which can be shaped into definite fashion. My pupils soon came to me, urged by this new necessity. What life requires that life provides, wherever life is or has been ; what youth requires that youth provides, wherever youth is or has been. And what the later man's life requires from a man, or from men in general, that also is provided by the boy's life and the youth's life when these have been genuinely lived through. The demand of my pupils set me upon the following question : " What did you do as a boy ? What happened to you to satisfy that need of yours for something to do and to express ? By what, at the same period of your life, was this need most fully met, or what did you then most desire for this purpose ? " Then there came to me a memory from out my earliest boyhood, which yielded me all I wanted in my emergency. It was the easy art of impressing figures and forms by properly arranged simple strokes on smooth paper.* I have often made use of this simple art in my later life, and have never found it fail in its object ; and on this occasion, too, it faithfully served my pupils and me, for our skill, at first weak both on the part of teacher and pupil, grew rapidly greater with use.

From these forms impressed upon paper we rose to making forms out of paper itself, and then to producing forms in pasteboard, and finally in wood. My later experience has taught me much more as to the best shapes and materials for the study of forms,† of which I shall speak in its proper place.

I must, however, permit myself to dwell a little upon this extremely simple occupation of impressing forms on paper, because at the proper age it quite absorbs a boy, and completely

---

* Probably done with the point of a knitting needle, etc. The design is then visible on the other side of the paper in an embossed form.

† This account is dated 1827, it is always necessary to remember.

fills and contents the demands of his faculties. Why is this? It gives the boy, easily and spontaneously, and yet at the same time imperceptibly, precise, clear, and many-sided results due to his own creative power.

Man is compelled not only to recognise Nature in her manifold forms and appearances, but also to understand her in the unity of her inner working, of her effective force. Therefore he himself follows Nature's methods in the course of his own development and culture, and in his games he imitates Nature at her work of creation. The earliest natural formations, the fixed forms of crystals, seem as if driven together by some secret power external to themselves ; and the boy in his first games gladly imitates these first activities of nature, so that by the one he may learn to comprehend the other. Does not the boy take pleasure in building, and what else are the earliest fixed forms of Nature but built-up forms? However, this indication that a higher meaning underlies the occupation and games which children choose out for themselves must for the present suffice. And since these spontaneous activities of children have not yet been thoroughly thought out from a high point of view, and have not yet been regarded from what I might almost call their cosmical and anthropological side, we may from day to day expect some philosopher to write a comprehensive and important book about them.* From the love, the attention, the continued interest and the cheerfulness with which these occupations are plied by children other important considerations also arise, of quite a different character.

A boy's game necessarily brings him into some wider or fuller relationship, into relationship with some more elevated group of

---

* After all, the work was left to Froebel himself to do. These words were written in 1827. The "Menschen Erziehung" of Froebel ("Education of Man"), which appeared the year before, had also touched upon the subject. In 1837 was founded the *Sonntags-Blatt* (*Sunday Journal*), to which many essays and articles on the subject were contributed by Froebel. The third volume ("Pädagogik") of Dr. Wichard Lange's complete edition of Froebel's works is largely made up of the *Sonntags-Blatt* articles. The whole Kindergarten system rests mainly on this higher view of children's play. It was further developed in his "Mutter- und Kose-Lieder" (Mother's Songs and Games"), in which his first wife assisted him. That appeared in 1843.

ideas. Is he building a house ?—he builds it so that he may dwell in it like grown-up people do, and have just such another cupboard, and so forth, as they have, and be able to give people things out of it just as they do. And one must always take care of this: that the child who receives a present shall not have his nature cramped and stunted thereby; according to the measure of how much he receives, so much must he be able to give away. In fact, this is a necessity for a simple-hearted child. Happy is that little one who understands how to satisfy this need of his nature, to give by producing various gifts of his own creation ! As a perfect child of humanity, a boy ought to desire to enjoy and to bestow to the very utmost, for he dimly feels already that he belongs to the whole, to the universal, to the comprehensive in Nature, and it is as part of this that he lives ; therefore, as such would he accordingly be considered and so treated. When he has felt this, the most important means of development available for a human being at this stage has been discovered. With a well-disposed child at such a time nothing has any value except as it may serve for a common possession, for a bond of union between him and his beloved ones. This aspect of the child's character must be carefully noticed by parents and by teachers, and used by them as a means of awakening and developing the active and presentative side of his nature ; wherefore none, not even the simplest gifts from a child, should ever be suffered to be neglected.

To sketch my first attempt as an educator in one phrase, I sought with all my powers to give my pupils the best possible instruction, and the best possible training and culture, but I was unable to fulfil my intentions, to attain my end, in the position I then occupied, and with the degree of culture to which I had myself attained.

As soon as this had become fully evident to me, it occurred to my mind that nothing else could be so serviceable to me as a sojourn for a time with Pestalozzi. I expressed my views on this head very decidedly, and accordingly, in the summer of 1808, it was agreed that I should take my three pupils with me to Yverdon.

So it soon afterwards came about I was teacher and scholar, educator and pupil, all at the same time.

If I were to attempt to put into one sentence all I expected to find at Yverdon, I should say it was a vigorous inner life amongst the boys and youths, quickening, manifesting itself in all kinds of creative activity, satisfying the manysidedness of man, meeting all his necessities, and occupying all his powers both mental and bodily. Pestalozzi, so I imagined, must be the heart, the life-source, the spiritual guide of this life and work; from his central point he must watch over the boy's life in all its bearings, see it in all its stages of development, or at all events sympathise with it and feel with it, whether as the life of the individual, of the family, of the community, of the nation, of mankind at large.

With such expectations I arrived at Yverdon. There was no educational problem whose resolution I did not firmly expect to find there. That my soul soon faithfully mirrored the life which there flowed around me, my report for 1809 sufficiently shows.*

To throw myself completely into the midst, into the very heart, of Pestalozzi's work, I wished to live in the main buildings of the institution, that is to say, in the castle itself.† We would have cheerfully shared the lot of the ordinary scholars, but our wish could not be granted, some outside jealousies standing in the way. However, I soon found a lodging in immediate prox-imity to the institution, so that we were able to join the pupils at their dinner, their evening meal, and their supper, and to take part in the whole courses of their instruction, so far as the subjects chosen by us were concerned; indeed, to share in their whole life. I soon saw much that was imperfect; but, notwith-standing, the activity which pressed forth on all sides, the vigorous effort, the spiritual endeavour of the life around me, which carried me away with it as it did all other men who came within its influence, convinced me that here I should pre-sently be able to resolve all my difficulties. As far as regarded

---

* A report that Froebel drew up for the Princess Regent of Rudolstadt in 1809, giving a voluminous account of the theory and practice pursued at Yverdon (Wichard Lange's "Froebel," vol. i., p. 154).

† The castle of Yverdon, an old feudal stronghold, which Pestalozzi had received from the municipality of that town in 1804, to enable him to establish a school and work out his educational system there.

myself personally, I had nothing more earnest to do for the time than to watch that my pupils gained the fullest possible profit from this life which was so rich in vigour for both body and soul. Accordingly we shared all lessons together; and I made it my special business to reason out with Pestalozzi each branch of instruction from its first point of connection with the rest, and thus to study it from its very root.

The forcible, comprehensive, stimulating life stimulated me too, and seized upon me with all its comprehensiveness and all its force. It is true it could not blind me to many imperfections and deficiencies, but these were retrieved by the general tendency and endeavour of the whole system; for this, though containing several absolute contradictions, manifest even at that time, yet vindicated on a general view its inner connection and hidden unity. The powerful, indefinable, stirring, and uplifting effect produced by Pestalozzi when he spoke, set one's soul on fire for a higher, nobler life, although he had not made clear or sure the exact way towards it, nor indicated the means whereby to attain it. Thus did the power and manysidedness of the educational effort make up for deficiency in unity and comprehensiveness; and the love, the warmth, the stir of the whole, the human kindness and benevolence of it replaced the want of clearness, depth, thoroughness, extent, perseverance, and steadiness. In this way each separate branch of education was in such a condition as to powerfully interest, but never wholly to content the observer, since it prepared only further division and separation and did not tend towards unity.

The want of unity of effort, both as to means and aims, I soon felt; I recognised it in the inadequacy, the incompleteness, and the unlikeness of the ways in which the various subjects were taught. Therefore I endeavoured to gain the greatest possible insight into all, and became a scholar in all subjects—arithmetic, form, singing, reading, drawing, language, physical geography, the natural sciences, etc.

I could see something higher, and I believed in a higher efficiency, a closer unity of the whole educational system; in truth, I believed I saw this clearer, though not with greater conviction, than Pestalozzi himself. I held that land happy, that man fortunate, by whom the means of true education should be developed and applied, and the wish to see this benefit conferred upon my country naturally sprang from the love I bore my native land.* The result was the written record of 1809 already referred to.

Where there is the germ of disunion, where the whole is split up, even sometimes into contradictory parts, and where an absolute reconciling unity is wanting, where what connection there may be is derived rather from casual outward ties than from inner necessary union, the whole system must of necessity dig its own grave, and become its own murderer. Now it was exactly at such a time of supreme crisis that I had the good or the evil fortune to be at Yverdon. All that was good and all that was bad, all that was profitable and all that was unprofitable, all that was strong and all that was weak, all that was empty and all that was full, all that was selfish and all that was unselfish amongst Pestalozzi and his friends, was displayed openly before me.

I happened to be there precisely at the time of the great Commission of 1810. Neither Pestalozzi nor his so-called friends, neither any individuals nor the whole community, could give me, or would give me, what I wanted. In the methods laid down by them for teaching boys, for the thorough education of boys as part of one great human family,—that is, for their higher instruction,— I failed to find that comprehensiveness which is alone sufficient to satisfy the human being. Thus it was with natural history, natural science, German, and language generally, with history, and above all, with religious instruction. Pestalozzi's devotional addresses were very vague, and, as experience showed, were only serviceable to those already in the right way.† I spoke of all these

---

* Froebel desired to see in Rudolstadt, or elsewhere in Thuringia (his " native land "), an institution like that of Pestalozzi at Yverdon ; and he sought to interest the Princess Regent of Rudolstadt by the full account of Yverdon already mentioned.

† This would scarcely seem probable to those who admire and love Pestalozzi. But we must remember that religious teaching appeals so intimately to individual sympathies that it is quite possible that what was of vital service to many others was not of so much use to Froebel, who was, as he frankly admits, out of harmony on many points with his noble-hearted teacher.

things very earnestly and decidedly with Pestalozzi, and at last I made up my mind, in 1810, to quit Yverdon along with my pupils.

But before I continue further here, it is my duty to consider my life and work from yet another point of view.

Amongst the various branches of education, the teaching of languages struck me with especial force as defective, on account of its great imperfection, its capriciousness and lifelessness. The search for a satisfactory method for our native language occupied me in preference to anything else. I proceeded on the following basis :—

Language is an image, a representation of our separate (subject) world, and becomes manifest to the (object) world outside ourselves principally through combined and ordered sounds. If, therefore, I would image forth anything correctly, I must know the real nature of the original object. The theme of our imagery and representation, the outside world, contains objects, therefore I must have a definite form, a definite succession of sounds, a definite word to express each object. The objects have qualities, therefore our language must contain adjectives expressing these qualities. The qualities of objects are fundamental or relative ; express what they are, what they possess, and what they become.

Passing now to singing and music, it happened very luckily for me that just at this time Nägeli and Pfeifer brought out their "Treatise on the Construction of a Musical Course according to the Principles of Pestalozzi." Nägeli's knowledge of music generally, and especially of church music, made a powerful impression upon me, and brought music and singing before me as a means for human culture ; setting the cultivation of music, and especially of singing, in a higher light than I had ever conceived possible. Nägeli was very capable in teaching music and singing, and in representing their function as inspiring aids to pure human life ; and although nearly twenty years have elapsed since I heard those lessons of his, the fire of the love for music which they kindled burns yet, active for good, within my breast. And further, I was taught and convinced by these two super-excellent music teachers, who instructed my pupils, that purely instrumental music, such as

6

that of the violin or of the pianoforte, is also in its essence based upon and derived from vocal music, though developed through the independent discovery of a few simple sound-producing instruments.   Not only have I never since left the path thus opened to me at its origin, but I have consistently traced it onwards in all care and love, and continue to rejoice in the excellent results obtained.   This course of music-teaching, as extended and applied later on, has always enjoyed the approbation of the thoughful and experienced amongst music teachers.

I also studied the boys' play, the whole series of games in the open air, and learned to recognise their mighty power to awake and to strengthen the intelligence and the soul as well as the body.   In these games and what was connected with them I detected the mainspring of the moral strength which animated the pupils and the young people in the institution.   The games, as I am now fervently assured, formed a mental bath of extraordinary strengthening-power ; * and although the sense of the higher symbolic meaning of games had not yet dawned upon me, I was nevertheless able to perceive in each boy genuinely at play a moral strength governing both mind and body which won my highest esteem.

Closely akin to the games in their morally strengthening aspect were the walks, especially those of the general walking parties, more particularly when conducted by Pestalozzi himself.   These walks were by no means always meant to be opportunities for drawing close to Nature, but Nature herself, though unsought, always drew the walkers close to her.   Every contact with her elevates, strengthens, purifies.   It is from this cause that Nature, like noble great-souled men, wins us to her ; and whenever school or teaching duties gave me respite, my life at this time was always passed amidst natural scenes and in communion with Nature. From the tops of the high mountains near by I used to rejoice in the clear and still sunset, in the pine-forests, the glaciers, the mountain meadows, all bathed in rosy light.   Such an evening walk

* That the boys' characters were immersed in an element of strengthening and developing games as the body is immersed in the water of a strengthening bath, seems to be Froebel's idea.

came indeed to be an almost irresistible necessity to me after each actively-spent day. As I wandered on the sunlit, far-stretching hills, or along the still shore of the lake, clear as crystal, smooth as a mirror, or in the shady groves, under the tall forest trees, my spirit grew full with ideas of the truly god-like nature and priceless value of a man's soul, and I gladdened myself with the consideration of mankind as the beloved children of God. There is no question but that Pestalozzi's general addresses, especially those delivered in the evening, when he used to delight in evoking a picture of noble manliness and true love of mankind and developing it in all its details, very powerfully contributed towards arousing such an inner life as that just described.

Yet I did not lose myself in empty fancies ; on the contrary, I kept my practical work constantly before my eyes. From thinking about my dead parents my thoughts would wander back over the rest of my family, turning most often to that dear eldest brother of mine, who has now not been referred to for some time in these pages. He had become the faithful watchful father of several children. I shared in his unaffected fatherly cares, and my soul was penetrated with the desire that he might be able to give his sons such an education as I should feel obliged to point out to him as being the best. Already, ever since I was at Frankfurt, I had communicated to him my thoughts on education and methods of teaching. What now occurred to me out of my new knowledge as applicable to his case, I extracted, collected together, and classified, so as to be able to impart it to him for his use at the first opportunity.

One thing which greatly contributed to the better consideration and elucidation of the Pestalozzian mode of teaching was the presence of a large number of young men sent from various governments as students to Yverdon. With some of these I was on terms of intimacy, and to the exchange of ideas which went on amongst us I owe at least as much as to my own observation.

On the whole I passed a glorious time at Yverdon, elevated in tone, and critically decisive for my after life. At its close, however, I felt more clearly than ever the deficiency of inner unity and interdependence, as well as of outward comprehensiveness and thoroughness in the teaching there.

To obtain the means of a satisfactory judgment upon the best method of teaching the classical tongues, I took Greek and Latin under a young German, who was staying there at that time ; but I was constructing a method of my own all the while, by observing all the points which seemed valuable, as they occurred in actual teaching. But the want of a satisfactory presentation of the classical tongues as part of the general means of education and culture of mankind, especially when added to the want of a consideration of natural history as a comprehensive and necessary means of education, and above all the uncertain wavering of the ground-principles on which the whole education and teaching rested at Yverdon, decided me not only to take my pupils back to their parents' house, but to abandon altogether my present educational work, in order to equip myself, by renewed study at some German university, with that due knowledge of natural science which now seemed to me quite indispensable for an educator.

In the year 1810 I returned from Yverdon by Bern, Schaffhausen, and Stuttgart to Frankfurt.

I should have prepared to go to the university at once, but found myself obliged to remain at my post till the July of the following year. The piece-meal condition of the methods of teaching and of education which surrounded me hung heavy on my mind, so that I was extremely glad when at last I was able to shake myself free from my position.

In the beginning of July 1811 I went to Göttingen. I went up at once, although it was in the middle of the session, because I felt that I should require several months to see my way towards harmonising my inward with my outward life, and reconciling my thoughts with my actions. And it was in truth several months before I gained peace within myself, and before I arrived at that unity which was so necessary to me, between my inward and my outward life, and at the equally necessary harmony between aim, career, and method.

Mankind as a whole, as one great unity, had now become my quickening thought. I kept this conception continually before my mind. I sought after proofs of it in my little world within, and in the great world without me ; I desired by many a struggle to win it, and then to set it worthily forth. And thus I was led back to the first appearance of man upon our earth, to the land which first saw man, and to the first manifestation of mankind, his speech.

Linguistic studies, the learning of languages, philology, etc., now formed the object of my attack. The study of Oriental tongues seemed to me the central point, the fountain head, whither my search was leading me ; and at once I began upon them with Hebrew and Arabic. I had a dim idea of opening up a path through them to other Asiatic tongues, particularly those of India * and Persia. I was powerfully stimulated and attracted by what I had heard about the study of these languages, then in its early youth—namely, the acknowledgment of a relationship between Persian and German. Greek also attracted me in quite a special way on account of its inner fulness, organisation, and regularity. My whole time and energy were devoted to the two languages I have named.† But I did not get far with Hebrew in spite of my genuine zeal and my strict way with myself, because between the manner of looking at a language congenial to my mind and the manner in which the elementary lesson book presented it to me, lay a vast chasm which I could find no means to bridge over. In the form in which language was offered to me, I could find and see no means of making it a living study ; and yet, nevertheless, nothing would have drawn me from my linguistic studies had I not been assured by educated men that these studies, especially my work on Indian and Persian tongues, were in reality quite beside the mark at which I aimed. Hebrew also was abandoned ; but, on the other hand, Greek irresistibly enthralled me, and nearly all my time and energy were finally given to its study, with the help of the best books.

I was now free, happy, in good mental and bodily health and vigour, and I gained peace within myself and without, through hard work, interrupted only by an indisposition which kept me to my room for a few weeks. After working all day alone, I used to walk out late in the evening, so that at least I might receive a greeting from the friendly beams of the setting sun. To in-

---

* Sanskrit is here probably meant.
† Hebrew and Arabic.

vigorate my spirit as well as my bodily frame I would walk on till near midnight in the beautiful neighbourhood which surrounds Göttingen. The glittering starry sky harmonised well with my thoughts, and a new object which appeared in the heavens at this time, aroused my wonder in an especial degree. I knew but little of astronomy, and the expected arrival of a large comet * was, therefore, quite unknown to me; so that I found out the comet for myself, and that was a source of special attraction. This object absorbed my contemplation in those silent nights, and the thought of the all-embracing, wide-spreading sphere of law and order above, developed and shaped itself in my mind with especial force during my night-wanderings. I often turned back home that I might note down in their freshness the results of these musings; and then after a short sleep I rose again to pursue my studies.

In this way the last half of the summer session passed quickly away, and Michaelmas arrived.

The development of my inner life had meanwhile insensibly drawn me little by little quite away from the study of languages, and led me towards the deeper-lying unity of natural objects. My earlier plan gradually reasserted itself, to study Nature in her first forms and elements. But the funds which still remained to me were now too small to permit of the longer residence at the university which that plan necessitated. As I had nothing at all now to depend upon save my own unaided powers, I at first thought to gain my object by turning them to some practical account, such as literary work. I had already begun to prepare for this, when an unexpected legacy changed my whole position. Up to now I had had one aunt still living, a sister of my mother's, who had spent all the best years of her life in my native village, enjoying excellent health and free from care. By her sudden

---

* The comet of 1811, one of the most brilliant of the present century, was an equal surprise to the most skilled astronomers as to Froebel. Observations of its path have led to a belief that it has a period of 300 years; so that it was possibly seen by our ancestors in 1511, and may be seen by our remote descendants in 2111. The appearance of this comet was synchronous with an unusually fine vintage harvest, and "wine of the great Comet year" was long held in great esteem.

death I obtained, in a manner I had little expected, the means of pursuing my much-desired studies. This occurrence made a very deep impression upon me, because this lady was the sister of that uncle of mine whose death had enabled me to travel from Gross Milchow to Frankfurt, and so first set me upon my career as an educator. And now again the death of a loved one made it possible for me to attain higher culture in the service of this career. Both brother and sister had loved with the closest affection my own mother, dead so far too soon, and this love they had extended to her children after her. May these two loving and beloved ones who through their death gave me a higher life and a higher vocation, live for ever through my work and my career.

My position was now a very pleasant one, and I felt soothing and cheering influences such as had not visited me before.

In the autumn holidays, too, a friendly home was ready to receive me. Besides the country-clergyman brother, who so often was a power for good in my life, I had another brother, also older than I, who had been living more than ten years as a well-established tradesman and citizen in Osterode, amongst the Harz Mountains; head of a quiet, self-contained, happy family, and father of some fine children. My previous life and endeavours as an educator had already brought me into connection with this circle; for I had not failed whenever I found anything suitable to my brother's needs to let him know of it, as he was the conscientious teacher and educator of his own children. It was in this peaceful, active family-circle of an intellectual tradesman's home that I passed all the vacation time during which the university regulations released me from vigorous work. It could not prove otherwise than that such a visit should be of the greatest service to me in my general development, and I remember it with thankfulness even yet on that account.

I return now to my university life. Physics, chemistry, mineralogy, and natural history in general, were my principal studies.

The inner law and order embracing all things, and in itself conditioned and necessitated, now presented itself to me in such clearness that I could see nothing either in nature or in life in which it was not made manifest, although varying greatly according to its several manifestations, in complexity and in gradation. Just at this time those great discoveries of the French and English philosophers became generally known through which the great manifold external world was seen to form a comprehensive outer unity. And the labours of the German and Swedish philosophers to express these essentially conditioned fundamental laws in terms of weight and number, so that they might be studied and understood in their most exact expression, and in their mutual interchange and connection, fitted in exactly with my own longings and endeavours. Natural science and natural researches now seemed to me, while themselves belonging to a distinct plane of vital phenomena, the foundation and cornerstones which served to make clear and definite the laws and the progress of the development, the culture, and the education of mankind.

It was but natural that such studies should totally absorb me, occupy my whole energies, and keep me most busily employed. I studied chemistry and physics with the greatest possible zeal, but the teaching of the latter did not satisfy me so thoroughly as that of the former.

What in the current half-year's term I was regarding rather from a theoretical standpoint, I intended in the next half-year to study practically as a factor of actual life : hence I passed to organic chemistry and geology.* Those laws which I was able to observe in Nature I desired to trace also in the life and proceedings of man, wherefore I added to my previous studies history, politics, and political economy. These practical departments of knowledge brought vividly home to me the great truth that the most valuable wealth a man can possess lies in a cultivated mind, and in its suitable exercise upon matters growing out of its own natural conditions. I saw further that wealth arose quite as much from vigour of production as from saving by economical use ; and that those productions were the most valuable of all, which were the outcome and representation of lofty ideas or remarkable thoughts ; and finally, that politics itself was in its essence but a means of uplifting man from the necessities of Nature and of life to the freedom of the spirit and the will.

---

* *Geognosie.*

While I received much benefit from the lectures on natural history at the university, I could not fall in with the views held there as to fixed forms—crystallography, mineralogy, and natural philosophy. From what I had heard of the natural history lectures of Professor Weiss in Berlin, I felt sure that I could acquire a correct view of both these subjects from him. And also since my means would not allow me to stay even so long as one entire session more at Göttingen, whilst on the other hand I might hope at Berlin to earn enough by teaching to maintain a longer university career there, I came to the conclusion to go to Berlin at the beginning of the next winter session to study mineralogy, geology, and crystallography under Weiss, as well as to do some work at physics and physical laws.

After a stay of a few weeks with my brother at Osterode, I went to Berlin in October 1812.

The lectures for which I had so longed really came up to the needs of my mind and soul, and awakened in me, more fervent than ever, the certainty of the demonstrable inner connection of the whole cosmical development of the universe. I saw also the possibility of man's becoming conscious of this absolute unity of the universe, as well as of the diversity of things and appearances which is perpetually unfolding itself within that unity; and then, when I had made clear to myself, and brought fully home to my consciousness, the view that the infinitely varied phenomena in man's life, work, thought, feeling, and position, were all summed up in the unity of his personal existence, I felt myself able to turn my thoughts once more to educational problems.

To make sure of my power to maintain myself at the university, I undertook some teaching at a private school of good reputation.* My work here, beyond the sufficient support it afforded me during residence, had no positive effect upon the endeavour of my life, for I found neither high intelligence, lofty aims, nor unity in the course of instruction.

---

* The Plamann School, an institution of considerable merit. Plamann was a pupil of Pestalozzi. One of the present writers studied crystallography later on with a professor who had been a colleague of Froebel's in this same school, and who himself was also a pupil of Pestalozzi.

The fateful year 1813 had now begun. All men grasped weapons, and called on one another to fly to arms to defend the Fatherland. I, too, had a home, it is true, a birthplace, I might say a Motherland, but I could not feel that I had a Fatherland.* My home sent up no cry to me; I was no Prussian,† and thus it came about that the universal call to arms (in Berlin) affected me, in my retired life, but little. It was quite another sentiment which drew me to join the ranks of German soldiers; my enthusiasm was possibly small, but my determination was firmly fixed as the rocks themselves.

This sentiment was the consciousness of a pure German brotherhood, which I had always honoured in my soul as a lofty and sublime ideal; one which I earnestly desired might make itself felt in all its fulness and freedom all over Germany.

Besides the fidelity with which I clung to my avocation as an educator also influenced my action in this matter. Even if I could not say truly that I had a Fatherland, I must yet acknowledge that every boy, that every child, who might perhaps later on come to be educated by me would have a Fatherland, that this Fatherland was now requiring defence, and that the child was not in a position to share in that defence. It did not seem possible to imagine that a young man capable of bearing arms could become a teacher of children and boys whose Fatherland he had refused to defend with his blood and even with his life if need were; that he who now did not feel ashamed to shrink from blows could exist without blushing in after years, or could incite his pupils to do something noble, something calling for sacrifice

---

* Froebel is here symbolically expressing the longing which pervaded all noble spirits at that time for a free and united Germany, for a great Fatherland. The tender mother's love was symbolised by the ties of home (Motherland), but the father's strength and power (Fatherland) was only then to be found in German national life in the one or two large states like Prussia, etc. It needed long years and the termination of this period of preparation by two great wars, those of 1866 and of 1870, to bind the whole people together, and make Germany no longer a "geographical expression" but a mighty nation.

† In the beginning of this great contest it was Prussia who declared war against the common enemy and oppressor, Napoleon. The other German powers, for the most part, held aloof.

and for unselfishness, without exposing himself to their derision and contempt. Such was the second main reason which influenced me.

Thirdly, this summons to war seemed to me an expression of the general need of the men, the land, and the times amidst which I lived, and I felt that it would be altogether unworthy and unmanly to stand by without fighting for this general need, and without taking my share in warding off the general danger.

Before these convictions all considerations gave way, even that of my bodily constitution, which was far too weakly for such a life.

As comrades I selected the Lützowers; and at Eastertide 1813 I arrived at Dresden on my road to join the infantry division of Lützow's corps at Leipzig.* Through the retired nature of my self-concentrated life it came about naturally that I, although a regularly matriculated student, had held aloof from the other students, and had gained no settled acquaintance amongst them; thus, out of all the vigorous comrades whom I met at Dresden, many of whom were like myself, Berlin students, I did not find one man I knew. I made but few new friends in the army, and these few I was fated to encounter on the first day of my entrance into my new work of soldiering. Our sergeant at the first morning halt after our march out from Dresden, introduced me to a comrade from Erfurt as a Thüringer, and therefore a fellow-countryman. This was Langethal; and casually as our acquaint-

---

* The Baron von Lützow formed his famous volunteer corps in March 1813. His instructions were to harass the enemy by constant skirmishes, and to encourage the smaller German states to rise against the tyrant Napoleon. The corps became celebrated for swift, dashing exploits in small bodies. Froebel seems to have been with the main body, and to have seen little of the more active doings of his regiment. Their favourite title was "Lützow's Wilde Verwegene Schaar" (Lützow's Wild Bold Troop). Amongst the volunteers were many distinguished men; for instance, the poet Körner, whose volume of war poetry, much of it written during the campaign, is still a great favourite. One of the poems, "Lützow's Wilde Jagd" ("Lützow's Wild Chase"), is of world-wide fame through the musical setting of the great composer Weber. In June 1813 came the armistice of which Froebel presently speaks. During the fresh outbreak of war after the armistice the corps was cut to pieces. It was reorganised, and we find it on the Rhine in December of the same year. It was finally dissolved after Napoleon's abdication and exile to Elba, 20th April, and the peace of Paris 30th May, 1814.

ance thus began, it proved to be a lasting friendship. Our first day's march was to Meissen, where we halted. We had enjoyed lovely spring weather during our march, and our repose was gladdened by a still lovelier evening. I found all the university students of the corps, driven by a like impulse, collected together in an open place by the shores of Elbe and near a public restaurant ; and some old Meissen wine soon served us as a bond of union. We sat about twenty strong in a jolly group at a long table, and began by welcoming and pledging one another to friendship. It was here that Langethal introduced me to a university friend of his at Berlin, the young Middendorff, a divinity student from the Mark.* Keeping together in a merry little society till the middle of the lovely spring night, we united again next morning in a visit to the splendid cathedral of Meissen. Thus from the very first did we three join fast in a common struggle towards and on behalf of the higher life, and even if we have not always remained in the like close outward bonds of union, we have from that time to this, now near upon fifteen years, never lost our comradeship in the inner life and our common endeavour after self-education. Both Langethal and Middendorff had a third friend, named Bauer, amongst our comrades of the camp. With him also, as I think, I made acquaintance as early as at Meissen, but it was more particularly at Havelberg, later on, that Bauer and I struck up a friendship together, which has ever since endured. Even when we have not been together in outward life, we have always remained one in our endeavours after the highest and best.

---

* *Die Grafschaft Mark.* The Mark of Brandenburg (so called as being the mark or frontier against Slavic heathendom in that direction during the dark ages) is the kernel of the Prussian monarchy. It was in the character of Markgraf of Brandenburg, that the Hohenzollern princes were electors of the German Empire ; their title as king was due not to Brandenburg, but to the dukedom of Prussia in the far east (once the territory of the Teutonic military order), which was elevated to the rank of an independent kingdom in 1701. The title of the present Emperor of Germany still begins "William, Emperor of Germany, King of Prussia, Markgraf of Brandenburg," etc., etc., showing the importance attached to this most ancient dignity. The Mark of Brandenburg contains Berlin. Middendorff seems to have been then living in the Mark. Froebel cannot have forgotten that by origin Wilhelm Middendorff was a Westphalian

Bauer closed the narrow circle of my friends amongst our companions in arms.*

I remained true to my previous way of life and thought in the manner in which I viewed my new soldier life. My main care was always to educate myself for the actual calling which at the moment I was following; thus, amongst the first things I took in hand was an attempt at finding the inner necessity and connection of the various parts of the drill and the military services, in which, without any previous acquaintance with military affairs, I managed, in consequence of my mathematical and physical knowledge, to succeed very fairly and without any great difficulty. I was able to protect myself, therefore, against many small reprimands, which fell tolerably frequently on those who had thought this or that instruction might be lightly passed over as too trivial to be attended to. It came about in this way, when we were continually drilling, after the cessation of the armistice, that the military exercises we performed gave me genuine pleasure on account of their regularity, their clearness, and the precision of their execution. In probing into their nature I could see freedom beneath their recognised necessity.

During the long sojourn of our corps in Havelberg previously alluded to, I strengthened my inner life, so far as the military service permitted, by spending all the time I could in the open

---

* Of Bauer little further is to be known. He was afterwards professor in the Frederick-William Gymnasium (Grammar School) in Berlin, but has no further connection with Froebel's career. On the other hand, a few words on Langethal and Middendorff seem necessary here. Heinrich Langethal was born in Erfurt, September 3rd, 1792. He joined Froebel at Keilhau in 1817. He was a faithful colleague of Froebel's there, and at Willisau and Burgdorf, but finally left him at the last place, and undertook the management of a girls' school at Bern. He afterwards became a minister in Schleusingen, returning eventually to Keilhau. One of the present writers saw him there in 1871. He was then quite blind, but happy and vigorous, though in his eightieth year. He died in 1879. Wilhelm Middendorff, the closest and truest friend Froebel ever had, without whom, indeed, he could not exist, because each formed the complement of the other's nature, was born at Brechten, near Dortmund, in Westphalia, September 20th, 1793, and died at Keilhau November 27th, 1853, a little over a year after his great master. (Froebel had passed away at Marienthal June 21st, 1852.)

air, in communion with Nature, to a perception of whose loveliness a perusal of G. Forster's "Travels in Rhineland" had newly unlocked my senses.*

We friends took all opportunities of meeting one another. By-and-by we set to work to make this easier by three of us applying to be quartered together.

In the rough, frank life of war, men presented themselves to me under various aspects, and so became a special object of my thoughts as regards their conduct, and their active work, and most of all as to their higher vocation. Man and the education of man was the subject which occupied us long and often in our walks, and in our open-air life generally. It was particularly these discussions which drew me forcibly towards Middendorff, the youngest of us.

I liked well our life of the bivouac, because it made so much of history clear to me ; and taught me, too, through our oft-continued and severely laborious marches and military manœuvres, the interchanging mutual relations of body and spirit. It showed me how little the individual man belongs to himself in war time ; he is but an atom in a great whole, and as such alone must he be considered.

Through the chance of our corps being far removed from the actual seat of war, we lived our soldier life, at least I did, in a sort of dream, notwithstanding the severe exertions caused by our military manœuvres, and we heard of the war only in the same sleepy way. Now and then, at Leipzig, at Dalenburg, at Bremen,

---

* "Ansichten vom Nieder Rhein, Flandern, Holland, England, Frankreich in April, Mai, und Juni 1790" ("Sketches on the Lower Rhine, Flanders,"etc.). Johann Georg Forster (1754—1794), the author of this book, accompanied his father, the naturalist, in Captain Cook's journey round the world. He then settled in Warrington (England) in 1767 ; taught languages, and translated many foreign books into English, etc. He left England in 1777, and served many princes on the Continent as librarian, historiographer, etc., amongst others the Czarina Catherine. He was librarian to the Elector of Mainz when the French Revolution broke out, and was sent as a deputation to Paris by the republicans of that town, who desired union with France. He died at Paris in 1794. His prose is considered classical in Germany, having the lightness of French and the power of English gained through his large knowledge of those literatures.

at Berlin, we seemed to wake up ; but soon sank back into feeble
dreaminess again.   It was particularly depressing and weakening
to me never to be able to grasp our position as part of the great
whole of the campaign, and never to find any satisfactory explanation of the reason or the aim of our manœuvres.   That was my
case at least ; others may have seen better and clearer than I.

I gained one clear benefit from the campaign ; in the course of
the actual soldier life I became enthusiastic upon the best interests
of the German land and the German people ; my efforts tended to
become national in their scope.   And in general, so far as my
fatigues allowed, I kept the sense of my future position always
before me ; even in the little skirmishes that we had to take part
in I was able to gather some experiences which I saw would be
useful to me in my future work.

Our corps marched through the Mark,* and in the latter part of
August through Priegnitz, Mecklenburg, the districts of Bremen
and Hamburg, and Holstein, and in the last days of 1813 we
reached the Rhine.   The peace (May 30th, 1814) prevented us
from seeing Paris, and we were stationed in the Netherlands till
the breaking up of the corps.   At last, in July 1814, every one
who did not care to serve longer had permission to return to his
home and to his former calling.   Upon my entrance into a corps
of Prussian soldiers I had received, through the influence of some
good friends, the promise of a post under the Prussian Government—namely, that of assistant at the mineralogical museum of
Berlin, under Weiss.   Thither then, as the next place of my
destined work, I turned my steps.   I desired also to see the
Rhine and the Main, and my birthplace as well ; so I went by
Düsseldorf back to Lünen, and thence by Mainz, Frankfurt, and
Rudolstadt to Berlin.

Thus I had lived through the whole campaign according to my
strength, greater or less, in a steady inner struggle towards unity
and harmony of life, but what of outward significance and worth
recollection had I received from the soldier's life ?   I left the
army and the warlike career with a total feeling of discontent.
My inner yearning for unity and harmony, for inward peace,

---

* The Mark of Brandenburg.

was so powerful that it shaped itself unconsciously into symbolical form and figure. In a ceaseless, inexplicable, anxious state of longing and unrest, I had passed through many pretty places and many gardens on my homeward way, without any of them pleasing me. In this mood I reached F——, and entered a fairly large and handsomely-stocked flower garden. I gazed at all the vigorous plants and fresh gay flowers it offered me, but no flower took my fancy. As I passed all the many varied beauties of the garden in review before my mind, it fell upon me suddenly that I missed the lily. I asked the owner of the garden if he had no lilies there, and he quietly replied, *No !* When I expressed my surprise, I was answered as quietly as before that hitherto no one had missed the lily. It was thus that I came to know what I missed and longed for. How could my inner nature have expressed itself more beautifully in words ? " Thou art seeking silent peacefulness of heart, harmony of life, clear purity of soul, by the symbol of this silent, pure, simple lily." That garden, in its beautiful variety, but without a lily, appeared to me as a gay life passed through and squandered without unity and harmony. Another day I saw many lovely lilies blooming in the garden of a house in the country. Great was my joy ; but, alas ! they were separated from me by a hedge. Later on I solved this symbol also ; and until its solution image and longing remained stored in my memory. One thing I ought to notice—namely, that in the place where I was vainly seeking for lilies in the garden a little boy of three years old came up trustfully and stood by my side.

I hastened to the scene of my new duties. How variously the different outward circumstances of my life henceforth affected me as to the life within, now that this had won for itself once more an assured individual form, and how my life again resumed its true and highest aspect, I must pass over here, since to develop these considerations with all their connections would take me too long. ·

In the first days of August 1814 I arrived at Berlin, and at once received my promised appointment. My duties busied me the greater part of the day amongst minerals, dumb witnesses to the silent thousand-fold creative energy of Nature, and I had to see to their arrangement in a locked, perfectly quiet room. While engaged on this work I continually proved to be true what had long been a presentiment with me—namely, that even in these so-called lifeless stones and fragments of rock, torn from their original bed, there lay germs of transforming, developing energy and activity. Amidst the diversity of forms around me, I recognised under all kinds of various modifications one law of development.

All the points that in Göttingen I had thought I traced amidst outward circumstances, confirmatory of the order of the soul's development, came before me here also, in a hundred and again a hundred phenomena. What I had recognised in things great or noble, or in the life of man, or in the ways of God, as serving towards the development of the human race, I found I could here recognise also in the smallest of these fixed forms which Nature alone had shaped. I saw clearly, as never yet I had seen before, that the godlike is not alone in the great; for the godlike is also in the very small, it appears in all its fulness and power in the most minute dimensions. And thereafter my rocks and crystals served me as a mirror wherein I might descry mankind, and man's development and history. These things began to stir powerfully within me ; and what I now vaguely perceived I was soon to view more definitely, and to be able to study with thoroughness.

Geology and crystallography not only opened up for me a higher circle of knowledge and insight, but also showed me a higher goal for my inquiry, my speculation, and my endeavour. Nature and man now seemed to me mutually to explain each other, through all their numberless various stages of development. Man, as I saw, receives from a knowledge of natural objects, even because of their immense deep-seated diversity, a foundation for, and a guidance towards, a knowledge of himself and of life, and a preparation for the manifestation of that knowledge. What I thus clearly perceived in the simpler natural objects I soon traced in the province of living Nature, in plants and growing things, so far as these came under my observation, and in the animal kingdom as well.

Soon I became wholly penetrated and absorbed by the thought that it must be beyond everything else vital to man's culture and development, to the sure attainment of his destiny and fulfilment

7

of his vocation, to distinguish these tendencies accurately and sharply not only in their separate ascending grades, but also throughout the whole career of life. Moreover, I made a resolution that for some time I would devote myself to the study of the higher methods of teaching, so as to fit myself as a teacher in one of the higher centres of education, as, for example, one of the universities, if that might be. But it was not long before I found a double deficiency, which quickly discouraged me in this design. For, firstly, I wanted a fund of specially learned and classical culture ; and next, I was generally deficient in the preparatory studies necessary for the higher branches of natural science. The amount of interest in their work shown by university students was, at the same time, not at all serious enough to attract me to such a career.

I soon perceived a double truth : first, that a man must be early led towards the knowledge of nature and insight into her methods—that is, he must be from the first specially trained with this object in view ; and next, I saw that a man, thus led through all the due stages of a life-development should in order to be quite sure to accomplish in all steadiness, clearness, and certainty his aim, his vocation, and his destiny, be guarded from the very beginning against a crowd of misconceptions and blunder. Therefore I determined to devote myself rather to the general subject of the education of man.

Though the splendid lectures I heard on mineralogy, crystallography, geology, etc., led me to see the uniformity of Nature in her working, yet a higher and greater unity lay in my own mind. To give an example, it was always most unsatisfactory to me to see form developed from a number of various ground-forms. The object which now lay before my efforts and my thought was to bring out the higher unity underlying external form in such a self-evident shape that it should serve as a type or principle whence all other forms might be derived. But as I held the laws of form to be fixed, not only for crystals, but also just as firmly for language, it was more particularly a deep philosophical view of language which eventually absorbed my thoughts. Again, ideas about language which I had conceived long ago in Switzerland crowded before my mind. It seemed to me that the vowels *a, o, u, e, i, ä, au, ei,* resembled, so to speak, force, spirit, the (inner) subject, whilst the consonants symbolised matter, body, the (outer) object. But just as in life and in nature all opposites are only relatively opposed, and within every circle, every sphere, both opposites are found to be contained, so also in language one perceives within the sphere of speech-tones the two opposites of subject and object. For example, the sound *i* depicts the absolute subject, the centre, and the sound *a* the absolute material object; the sound *e* serves for life as such, for existence in general; and *o* for individual life, for an existence narrowed to itself alone.

Language, not alone as the material for the expression of thought, but also as a type or epitome of all forms and manifestations of life, appeared to me to underlie the universal laws of expression. In order to learn these laws thoroughly, as exemplified in the teaching of the classical languages, I now returned again to the study of these latter, under the guidance of a clever teacher; and I began to strike out the special path which seemed to me absolutely necessary to be followed in their acquisition.

From this time onwards I gave all my thoughts to methods of education, whereto I was also further incited by some keen critical lectures on the history of ancient philosophy. These again afforded me a clear conviction of the soundness of my views of Nature and of the laws of human development.

Through my work at the dynamical, chemical, and mathematical aspects of Nature I came once more upon the consideration of the laws of number, particularly as manifested through figures; and this led me to a perfectly fresh general view of the subject— namely, that number should be regarded as horizontally related.* That way of considering the subject leads one to very simple fundamental conceptions of arithmetic, which, when applied in practice, prove to be as accurate as they are clear. The connection

---

* It is to be regretted that Froebel has not developed this point more fully He speaks of " die Betrachtung des Zahlensinnes in horizontaler oder Seiten-Richtung," and one would be glad of further details of this view of number. We think that the full expression of the thought here shadowed out, is to be found in the Kindergarten occupations of mat-weaving, stick-laying, etc., in their arithmetical aspect. Certainly in these occupations, instead of number being built up as with bricks, etc., it is laid along horizontally.

of these (dynamical and arithmetical) phenomena was demonstrably apparent to me ; since arithmetic may be considered, firstly, as the outward expression of the manifestation of force, secondly (in its relationship to man), as an example of the laws of human thought.

On all sides, through nature as well as through history, through life as well as through science (and as regards the latter through pure science as well as through the applied branches), I was thus encountered and appealed to by the unity, the simplicity, and the unalterably necessary course, of human development and human education. I became impelled by an irresistible impulse towards the setting forth of that unity and simplicity, with all the force, both of my pen and of my life, in the shape of an educational system. I felt that education as well as science would gain by what I may call a more human, related, affiliated, connected treatment and consideration of the subjects of education.

I was led to this conviction on another ground, as follows :— Although my friends Langethal, Middendorff, and Bauer served with me all through the war in the same corps, and even in the same battalion, we were a great deal apart towards the close of the campaign, especially at the time we were quartered in the Netherlands, so that I, at all events, at the disbanding of the corps, knew not whither the others had gone. It was, therefore, an unexpected pleasure when, after a while, I found them all at Berlin again. My friends pursued their theological studies with earnestness, and I my natural science ; therefore, at first we came little into contact with one another.

So passed several months, when suddenly life threw us closer together again. This came about through the call to arms in 1815. We all enlisted again together as volunteers. On account of our previous service, and by royal favour, we were at once promoted to officer's rank, and each one was appointed to a regiment. However, there was such a throng of volunteers that it was not necessary for any State officials to be called upon to leave their posts, or for students to interrupt their studies, and we therefore received counter-orders commanding us to stay at home. Middendorff, who felt sure of his speedy departure for the army, preferred not to take lodgings for the short time of his stay in Berlin, and as there was room enough in mine for us both, he came and stayed with me. Yet we still seemed to draw very little closer together at first, because of the diversity of our pursuits; but soon a bond of union wove itself again, which was all the stronger on that very account. Langethal and Middendorff had endeavoured to secure a sufficiency for their support at the university by taking private tutorships in families, making such arrangements as that their university studies should not be interfered with. In the beginning of their work all seemed simple and easy, but they soon came upon difficulties both as regards the teaching and the training of the children entrusted to them. As our former conversations had so often turned upon these very subjects they now came to me to consult me, especially about mathematical teaching and arithmetic, and we set apart two hours a week, in which I gave them instruction on these matters. From this moment our mutual interchange of thought again became animated and continuous.

✢　　*　　*　　*　　*　　*　　*

Here the autobiography breaks off abruptly. Herr Wichard Lange had some trouble in deciphering it from Froebel's almost unreadable rough draft, and here and there he had even to guess at a word or so. Froebel had intended to present this letter to the Duke of Meiningen at the close of 1827, when the negotiations began to be held about a proposed National Educational Institution at Helba, to be maintained by the duke, after the similar proposal made to the Prince of Rudolstadt for Quittelsdorf earlier in the year had broken down. It is not known whether the present draft was ever finished, properly corrected, and polished into permanent form, nor whether it was ever delivered to the duke. It is highly probable that we have here all that Froebel accomplished towards it. It may be added that soon after Froebel's repeated plans and drafts for the Helba Institution had culminated in the final extensive well-known plan of the spring of 1829, the whole scheme fell through, from the jealousy of the prince's advisers, who feared Froebel's influence too much to allow him ever to get a footing amongst them.

Another fragment of autobiography, going on to a further period of his life, occurs in a long letter to the philosopher Krause,* dated Keilhau, 24th March, 1828, in reply to an article written by Krause five years before (1823) in Oken's journal, the well-known *Isis,†* in which article Krause had found fault with Froebel's two explanatory essays on Keilhau, written in 1822, separately published, and appearing also in the *Isis*, because Keilhau was there put forward as "an educational institution for all Germany" (Allgemeine Deutsche Erziehungs-Anstalt), whereas Krause desired 't should rather style itself "a German institution for universal

---

* Carl Christian Friedrich Krause, an eminent philosopher, and the most learned writer on freemasonry in his day, was born in 1781, at Eisenberg, in Saxe-Altenburg. From 1801 to 1804 he was a professor at Jena, afterwards teaching in Dresden, Göttingen, and Munich, at which latter place he died in 1832.

† Lorenz Oken, the famous naturalist and man of science, was born at Rohlsbach, in Swabia, 1st August, 1779. (His real name was Ockenfuss.) In 1812 Oken was appointed ordinary professor of natural history at Jena, and in 1816 he founded his celebrated journal, the *Isis*, devoted chiefly to science, but also admitting comments on political matters. The latter having given

culture " (Deutsche Anstalt für Allgemeine menschliche Bildung). The rapid growth of Keilhau gave Froebel at the time no leisure for controversy. In 1827 began the cruel persecutions which eventually compelled him to leave Keilhau. Now whenever Froebel was under the pressure of outward difficulty, he always sought for help from within, and from his inward contemplation derived new courage and new strength to face his troubles. Out of such musings in the present time of adversity the long-awaited reply to Krause at length emerged. The disputative part, interesting in itself, does not here concern us. We pass at once to the brief sketch of his life contained in later parts of the letter, omitting what is not autobiographical. The earlier of these passages relate more succinctly the events of the same period already more fully described in the letter to the Duke of Meiningen; but we think it better to print the passages in full, in spite of their being to a great extent a repetition of what has gone before. Certain differences, however, will be found not unworthy of notice.

The Krause letter succeeded the other and more important letter (to the Duke of Meiningen) by some few months. Its immediate outcome was a warm friendship between Krause and Froebel; the latter, with Middendorff as his companion, journeying to Göttingen to make the philosopher's personal acquaintance, in the autumn of 1828. Long discussions on education took place at this interesting meeting, as we know from Leonhardi, Krause's pupil. Krause made Froebel acquainted with the works of Comenius, amongst other things, and introduced him to the whole learned society of Göttingen, where he made a great, if a somewhat peculiar, impression.

---

offence to the Court of Weimar, Oken was called upon either to resign his professorship or suppress the *Isis*. He chose the former alternative, sent in his resignation, transferred the publication of the *Isis* to Rudolstadt, and remained at Jena as a private teacher of science. In 1821 he broached in the *Isis* the idea of an annual gathering of German *savants*, and it was carried out successfully at Leipzig in the following year. To Oken, therefore, may be indirectly ascribed the genesis of the annual scientific gatherings common on the Continent, as well as of the British Association for the Advancement of Science, which at the outset was avowedly organised after his model. He died in 1851.

. . . You have enjoyed, without doubt, unusual good fortune in having pursued the strict path of culture. You have sailed by Charybdis without being swallowed up by Scylla.* But my lot has been just the reverse.

As I have already told you in the beginning of this letter, I was very early impressed with the contradictions of life in word and deed—in fact, almost as soon as I was conscious of anything, living as a lonely child in a very narrowed and narrowing circle. A spirit of contemplation, of simplicity, and of childlike faith ; a stern, sometimes cruel, self-repression ; a carefully-fostered inward yearning after knowledge by causes and effects, together with an open-air life amidst Nature, especially amidst the world of plants, gradually freed my soul from the oppression of these contradictions. Thus, in my tenth and eleventh years, I came to dream of life as a connected whole without contradictions. Everywhere to find life, harmony, freedom from contradictions, and so to recognise with a keener and clearer perception the life-unity after which I dimly groped, was the silent longing of my heart, the mainspring of my existence. But the way thither through the usual school course, all made up of separate patches, considering things merely in their outward aspect, and connected by mere arbitrary juxtaposition, was too lifeless to attract me ; I could not remember things merely put together without inner connection, and so it came about that after two of my elder brothers had devoted themselves to study, and because my third brother showed great capacity for study also, my own education was narrowed ;

---

* Those acquainted with the classical mythology will forgive us for noting that Charybdis was, and is, a whirlpool on the Sicilian shore of the Straits of Messina, face to face with some caverns under the rock of Scylla, on the Italian shore, into which the waves rush at high tide with a roar not unlike a dog's bark.

but so much the more closely did a loving, guiding providence bind my heart in communion with Nature.*

In silent, trustful association with Nature and my mathematics, I lived for several years after my confirmation. In the latter part of the time my duties led me towards the study of natural laws, and thus towards the perception of the unity so often longed for in soul and spirit, and now at last gradually becoming clear from amidst the outwardly clashing phenomena of Nature.†

At last I could no longer resist the craving for knowledge which I felt within me. I thrust on one side all the ordinary school-learning which I utterly failed to appropriate in its customary disconnected state (it was meant only to be learned by rote, and this I never could recognise as the exclusive condition of a really comprehensive culture of the human mind), and I went up in the middle of my eighteenth year to the University of Jena. As I had been for two years past living completely with Nature and my mathematics, and dependent upon myself alone for any culture I might have arrived at, I came to the university much like a simple plant of nature myself. I was at this time peculiarly moved by a little knowledge I had picked up about the solar system, including particularly a general conception of Kepler's laws, whereby the laws of the spheres appealed to me on the one hand as an all-embracing, world-encircling whole, and on the other as an unlimited individualisation into separate natural objects. My own culture had been hitherto left to myself, and so also now I had to select my own studies and to choose my courses of lectures for myself. It was to be expected that the lectures of

---

* The peculiar dreamy boy, who by his nature was set against much of his work, and therefore seemed but an idle fellow to his schoolmaster, was thought to be less gifted than his brothers, and on that account fitted not so much for study as for simple practical life. In Oberweissbach he was set down as "moonstruck." All this is more fully set forth in the Meiningen letter, and the footnotes to it.

† This was the time when he was apprenticed to the forester in Neuhaus, in the Thüringer Wald, and necessarily studied mathematics, nature, and the culture of forest trees. Eyewitnesses have described him as extremely peculiar in all his ways, even to his dress, which was often fantastic. He was fond of mighty boots and great waving feathers in his green hunter's-hat, etc.

the professors would produce a singular effect upon me, and so they did.

I chose as my courses natural history, physics, and mathematics, but I was little satisfied. I seldom gained what I expected. Everywhere I sought for a sound method deriving itself from the fundamental principle lying at the root of the subject in hand, and afterwards summing up all details into that unity again ; everywhere I sought for recognition of the quickening interconnection of parts, and for the exposition of the inner all-pervading reign of law. Only a few lectures made some poor approach to such methods, but I found nothing of the sort in those which were most important to me, physics and mathematics. Especially repugnant to me was the piece-meal patchwork offered to us in geometry, always separating and dividing, never uniting and consolidating.

I was, however, perfectly fascinated with the mathematical rules of "combination, permutation, and variation," but unhappily I could not give much time to their study, which I have regretted ever since. Otherwise, what I learned from the lectures was too slight for what I wanted, being, unluckily, altogether foreign to my nature, and more often a mere getting of rules by heart rather than an unfolding of principles. The theoretical and philosophical courses on various subjects did not attract me either, something about them always kept me at a distance ; and from what I heard of them amongst my fellow-students, I could gather that here, too, all was presented in an arbitrary fashion, unnaturally divided, cut up, so to speak, into lifeless morsels ; so that it was useless for my inner life to seek for satisfaction in those regions of study. But as I said above, there were some of the lectures which fostered my interest in the inner connection of all vital phenomena, and even helped me to trace it with some certainty in some few restricted circles.

But my financial position did not permit me to remain long at the university ; and as my studies were those which fitted the student for practical professional life, though they were regarded from a higher point of view by myself in the privacy of my own thoughts, I had to return to ordinary every-day work, and use them as a means to earn my living. Yet, though I lived the outward business life to all appearance, it remained ever foreign to my nature; I carried my own world within me, and it was that for which I cared and which I cherished. My observation of life (and especially that of my own life, which I pursued with the object of self-culture), joined with the love of Nature and with mathematics to work creatively upon me; and they united to fill my little mental world with many varied life-forms, and taught me at the same time to regard my own existence as one member of the great universal life. My plan of culture was very simple : it was to seek out the innermost unity connecting the most diverse and widely-separated phenomena, whether subjective or objective, and whether theoretical or practical, to learn to see the spiritual side of their activity, to apprehend their mutual relations as facts and forms of Nature, or to express them mathematically ; and, on the other hand, to contemplate the natural and mathematical laws as founded in the innermost depths of my own life as well as in the highest unity of the great whole, that is indeed to regard them in their unconditioned, uncaused necessity, as " absolute things-in-themselves." Thus did I continue without ceasing to systematise, symbolise, idealise, realise and recognise identities and analogies amongst all facts and phenomena, all problems, expressions, and formulas which deeply interested me , and in this way life, with all its varied phenomena and activities, became to me more and more free from contradictions, more harmonious, simple, and clear, and more recognisable as a part of the life universal.

After I had lived for some years the isolated life I have described, though I was engaged the whole time in ordinary professional pursuits, all at once there broke upon my soul, in harmony with the seasons of nature, a springtime such as I had not before experienced ; and an unexpected life and life-aim budded and blossomed in my breast. All my inner life and life-aims had become narrowed to the circle of self-culture and self-education. The outer life, my profession, I carried on as a mere means of subsistence, quite apart from my real inner self, and my sphere of operation was limited. I was driven perforce from pillar to post till at last I had arrived where the Main unites herself with the Rhine.* Here there budded and opened to my soul one lovely

* *i.e.*, Mainz.

bright spring morning, when I was surrounded by Nature at her loveliest and freshest, this thought, as it were by inspiration :— That there must exist somewhere some beautifully simple and certain way of freeing human life from contradiction, or, as I then spake out my thought in words, some means of restoring to man, himself, at peace internally ; and that to seek out this way should be the vocation of my life. And yet my life, to all appearance, my studies and my desires, belonged to my purely external vocation,* and to its external citizenlike relations ; and by no means to mankind at large, either regarded in itself or in its educational needs. Therefore this idea of mine was in such violent contrast with my actual life that it utterly surprised me. In fact, and perhaps greatly because of this contrast, the idea would undoubtedly have been quite forgotten, had not other circumstances occurred to revive it. On myself and on my life at the time it seemed to have not the slightest effect, and it soon passed from my memory. But later on in this same journey,† as I climbed down from the Wartburg, and turned round to look at the castle, there rushed upon me once more this thought of a higher educational vocation as my proper life-work ; and again, being so far removed from my actual external life, it only flashed upon me with a momentary effulgence an instant, and then sank. This, unconsciously to me, and therefore quite disregarded by me, was the real position of my inner life when I arrived at the goal of my journey, Frankfurt, from whence my life was so soon to develop so largely. My energies at the moment were devoted towards attaining some definite professional position for myself.‡ But in proportion as I began to examine my profession more closely in its practical aspect, so did it begin to prove insufficient of itself to satisfy me as the occupation of my life. Then there came to me the definite purpose of living and working at my profession rather to use it as a means to win some high benefit for mankind. §

---

* Architecture, etc., at this time.   † From Mecklenburg to Frankfurt.
‡ *i.e.*, as an architect.
§ His plan evidently was to use architecture, probably Gothic architecture, as a means of culture and elevation for mankind, and not merely to practise it to gain money.

The restlessness of youth, nay, that chance, rather, which has always lovingly guided me, threw me unexpectedly into relations with a man whose knowledge of mankind, and whose penetrating glance into my inner being turned me at our very first interview from the profession of an architect to that of a teacher and an educator, two spheres of work which had never previously occurred to me, still less had appeared to me as the future objects of my life.* But the very first time I found myself before thirty or forty boys from nine to eleven years old, for that was the class allotted to me to teach, I felt thoroughly at home. In fact, I perceived that I had at last found my long-missed life element; and as I wrote to my brother at the time, I was as well pleased as the fish in the water, I was inexpressibly happy. Yet here from the very first moment (and what a number of sacrifices had to be made, what a wealth of activity was poured out!) I had to give information, advice, and decisions on matters which hitherto I had not thought it necessary seriously to consider, and so also here, in my new position, I soon came to feel myself isolated, to stand alone.

I sought counsel where I had so often found it. I looked within myself and to Nature for help. Here my plan of culture, hitherto followed only for my own needs, came opportunely to my assistance. When I was consulted by others, I looked to Nature for the answer, and let Nature, life, spirit, and law speak for themselves through me; then the answer was not merely satisfactory. No! its simple, unhesitating confidence and youthful freshness gladdened and quickened the inquirer.

This was all well enough when universal human interests were concerned, but how about matters of instruction? I could, in fact, fairly confess that in many respects I had no title to call myself a cultured man, for hitherto all my culture had been fragmentary or imaginative.

Once again I found myself in conflict with my environment; for I could not possibly torture my scholars with what I myself had refused to be tortured with—namely, the learning by heart of disconnected rules. I was therefore compelled to strike out fresh

---

* It was in 1805 that Froebel was appointed by Gruner teacher in the Normal School at Frankfurt.

paths for myself, which indeed my post rendered a delightful task; because I not only had full liberty accorded me in this matter, but was even urged onwards in that direction by my duty, since the institution was a model school for the higher development of teaching. My past self-culture, self-teaching, and self-development, and my study of Nature and of life now stood me in good stead.

But this letter is not intended to contain the whole history of the development of my mind; and I will therefore pass quickly forward, just mentioning that from this time for six years onwards, during which I thrice completely changed the conditions of my life,* I held most earnestly by this same temper of mind and this same endeavour; and although I still always lived in isolation as to my personal inner life, yet I was at many points in full contact with the brisk mental effort and activity of that stirring time (1805 to 1810), as regards teaching, philosophy, history, politics, and natural science.†

But the nobler, the more varied, the more animating was the life surrounding me, and the more I found all without me, as also all within me, striving and tending towards harmony and unity, by so much the less could I longer be restrained from seeking out this unity, even should it be at the sacrifice of all that was dear to me, if need were for that. I was impelled to seek to develop this unity all bright and living within my own soul, and to contemplate it in definite, clear, and independent form, so that finally I might be able to set it forth in my actual life with sureness and certainty.

---

* 1. Teacher in the Model School. 2. Tutor to the sons of Herr von Holzhausen near Frankfurt. 3. A resident at Yverdon with Pestalozzi.

† Froebel was driven to Yverdon by the perusal of some of Pestalozzi's works which Gruner had lent him. He stayed with Pestalozzi for a fortnight, and returned with the resolve to study further with the great Swiss reformer at some future time. In 1807, he became tutor to Herr von Holzhausen's somewhat spoilt boys, demanded to have the entire control of them, and for this object their isolation from their family. The grateful parents, with whom Froebel was very warmly intimate, always kept the rooms in which he dwelt with his pupils exactly as they were at that time, in remembrance of his remarkable success with these boys. Madame von Holzhausen had extraordinary influence with Froebel, and he continued in

After nine years' interval I visited the university a second time; first (spring of 1810) at Göttingen, and then a year and a half later (autumn of 1811) at Berlin.*

I now began to pursue the study of languages. The linguistic treasures which recent discoveries had brought us from Asia excited my deepest interest wherever I came into contact with them.

But in general the means of acquiring languages were too life-less, too wanting in connection to be of any use to me; and the effort to work them out afresh in my own way, soon led me to a renewed study of Nature. Nature held me henceforth so fast that for years I was chained uninterruptedly to her study, though truly languages went on as a side-study during the time. Yet it was not as separate entities that I considered the phenomena I was working at; rather was it as parts of the great whole of natural life, and this also I regarded as reposing in one supreme unity together with all mankind; Nature and man, the two opposite mutually casting light upon each other and mirroring each other.

After the German war of the spring of 1813 had interrupted my studies at Berlin, and I had made acquaintance with a soldier's life, its need, and its habits in Lützow's corps, I returned in 1814 to my studies and to a scientific public post in Berlin. The care, the arrangement, and in part the investigation and explanation of crystals were the duties of my office. Thus I reached at last the central point of my life and life-aim, where productiveness and law, life, nature, and mathematics united all of them in the fixed crystalline form, where a world of symbols offered itself to the

---

constant correspondence with her. In 1808 Froebel and his pupils went to Yverdon, and remained till 1810. But the philosophic groundwork of Pestalozzi's system failed to satisfy him. Pestalozzi's work started from the external needs of the poorest people, while Froebel desired to found the columns supporting human culture upon theoretically reasoned grounds and upon the natural sciences. A remarkable difference existed between the characters of the two great men. Pestalozzi was diffident, acknowledged freely his mistakes, and sometimes blamed himself for them bitterly; Froebel never thought himself in the wrong, if anything went amiss always found some external cause for the failure, and in self-confidence sometimes reached an extravagant pitch.

* Either Froebel or his editor has made a blunder here. Froebel went to Göttingen in July 1811 (see p. 84), and to Berlin in October 1812 (see p. 89).

inner eye of the mind ; for I was appointed assistant to Weiss at the mineralogical museum of the Berlin University. *

For a long time it was my endeavour and my dearest wish to devote myself entirely to an academical career, which then appeared to me as my true vocation and the only solution of the riddle of my life; but the opportunities I had of observing the natural history students of that time, their very slight knowledge of their subject, their deficiency of perceptive power, their still greater want of the true scientific spirit, warned me back from this plan. On the other hand, the need of man for a life worthy of his manhood and of his species pressed upon me with all the more force, and, therefore, teaching and education again asserted themselves vigorously as the chief subjects occupying my thoughts. Consequently I was only able to keep my mind contented with the duties of my post for two years; and, meanwhile, the stones in my hand and under my eyes turned to living, speaking forms. The crystal-world, in symbolic fashion, bare unimpeachable witness to me, through its brilliant unvarying shapes, of life and of the laws of human life, and spake to me with silent yet true and readable speech of the real life of the world of mankind.

Leaving everything else, sacrificing everything else, † I was driven back upon the education of man, driven also to my refuge in Nature, wherein as in a mirror I saw reflected the laws of the development of being, which laws I was now to turn to account for the education of my race. My task was to educate man in

---

* At this time, however, the symbols of the inorganic world did not appeal to Froebel with the same force as those of the organic world. In a letter to Madame von Holzhausen, 31st March, 1831, he writes : " It is the highest privilege of natural forms or of natural life that they contain agreement and perfection within themselves as a whole class, while differing and filled with imperfection in particular individuals ; for look at the loveliest blooming fruit-tree, the sweetest rose, the purest lily, and your eye can always detect deficiencies, imperfections, differences in each one, regarded as a single phenomenon, a separate bloom ; and, further, the same want of perfection appears also in every single petal : on the other hand, wherever mathematical symmetry and precise agreement are found, *there is death.*"

† Not a figure of speech altogether ; for Froebel did really decline a professorship of mineralogy which was offered him at this time, in order to set forth on his educational career.

his true humanity, to educate man in his absolute being, according to the universal laws of all development.* Therefore, leaving Berlin, and laying down my office, I began late in the autumn of 1816 that educational work which, though it still takes its impulse from me and exists under my leadership, yet in its deepest nature is self-sufficient and self-conditioned.

Although I was not perhaps then capable of putting my convictions into words, I at once realised this work in my own mind as comprehensive and world-embracing in its nature, as an everlasting work to be evermore performed for the benefit of the whole human race ; yet I nevertheless linked it, and for this very reason, to my own personal life ; that is, since I had no children of my own, I took to me my dear nephews whom I most deeply loved, in order through them and with them to work out blessings for my home and my native land, for Schwarzburg and Thuringia, and so for the whole wide Fatherland itself.† The eternal

---

* That is, putting development into a formula—

Thesis⊤Antithesis
Synthesis.

The true synthesis is that springing from the thesis and its opposite, the antithesis. Another type of the formula is this—

Proposition⊤Counter-proposition
Compromise.

Understanding by " Compromise " (*Vermittlung*) that which results from the union of the two opposites, that which forms part of both and which links them together. The formula expressed in terms of human life, for example, is—

Father⊤Mother
Child.

Philosophic readers acquainted with Hegel and his school will recognise a familiar friend in these formulæ.

† Froebel travelled from Berlin to Osterode, and took with him both his brother Christian's sons, Ferdinand and Wilhelm, to Griesheim ; there to educate them together with the three orphans of his brother Christoph, who had died in 1813, of hospital fever, whilst nursing the French soldiers. Of the sons of Christian, Ferdinand studied philosophy, and at his death was director of the Orphanage founded by Froebel in Burgdorf; Wilhelm, who showed great talent, and was his uncle's favourite nephew, died early through the consequences of an accident, just after receiving his " leaving certificate " from the gymnasium of Rudolstadt.

As regards the sons of Christoph, they were the immediate cause of Froebel's going to Griesheim, for their widowed mother sent for her brother-in

principles of development, as I recognised them within me, would have it thus and not otherwise.

Timidly, very timidly, did I venture to call my work by the title of "German," or "Universal German" education; and, indeed, I struck that out from one of my manuscripts, although it was precisely the name required to start with as it expressed the broad nature of my proposed institution. An appeal to the general public to become thorough *men* seemed to me too grandiose, too liable to be misunderstood, as, indeed, in the event, it only too truly proved; but to become thorough Germans, so I thought, would seem to them something in earnest, something worth the striving for, especially after such hard and special trials as had recently been endured by the German nation.

With your penetrating judgment you quarrelled with that term "German education;" but, after all, even the appeal to be made thorough Germans proved to be too grandiose and liable to be misunderstood. For every one said "German? Well, I *am*

---

law to consult him as to their education. Julius, the eldest, was well prepared in Keilhau for the active life he was afterwards destined to live. He went from school to Munich, first, to study the natural sciences; and while yet at the university several publications from his pen were issued by Cotta. Later on he took an official post in Weimar, and continued to write from time to time. Meanwhile he completed his studies in Jena and Berlin under Karl von Ritter, the great authority on cosmography, and under the distinguished naturalist, Alexander von Humboldt. In 1833 he became Professor at the Polytechnic School in Zürich; but his literary avocations eventually drew him to Dresden. Here he was chosen Deputy to the National Assembly at Frankfurt in 1848. After the dissolution of that Assembly, Julius Froebel, in common with many others of the more advanced party, was condemned to death. He escaped to Switzerland before arrest, and fled to New York. In after life he was permitted to return to Germany, and eventually he was appointed Consul at Smyrna.

Karl Froebel, the next son, went to Jena also. He then took a tutorship in England, and it was at this time (1831) that his pamphlet, "A Preparation for Euclid," appeared. He returned to the Continent to become Director of the Public Schools at Zürich. He left Zürich in 1848 for Hamburg, where he founded a Lyceum for Young Ladies. Some years later, when this had ceased to exist, he went again to England, and eventually founded an excellent school at Edinburgh with the aid of his wife; which, indeed, his wife and he still conduct. His daughters show great talent for music, and one of them was a pupil of the distinguished pianist, Madame Schumann (widow of the great composer).

German, and have been so from my birth, just as a mushroom is a mushroom ; what, then, do I want with education to teach me to be a thorough German ? " What would these worthy people have said, had I asked them to train themselves to become thorough men ? Now had I planned my educational institute altogether differently, had I offered to train a special class, body-servants, footmen or housemaids, shoemakers or tailors, trades-men or merchants, soldiers or even noblemen, then should I have gained fame and glory for the great usefulness and practical nature of my institution, for certain ; and surely all men would have hastened to acknowledge it as an important matter, and as a thing to be adequately supported by the State. I should have been held as the right man in the right place by the State and by the world ; and so much the more because as a State-machine I should have been engaged in cutting out and modelling other State-machines. But I—I only wanted to train up free, thinking, independent men ! Now who wants to be, or who cares to suffer another to be, a free-thinking, independent man ? If it was folly to talk about educating persons as Germans, what was it to talk about educating them as men ? The education of Germans was felt to be something extraordinary and farfetched ; the education of men was a mere shadow, a deceitful image, a blind enthusiasm.

From this digression I now return, to continue my attempt at making myself known to you, as far as is possible, in a letter ; by which I mean my real inner self, as manifested in my endeavours and my hopes.

Permit me, therefore, to go a step nearer towards what lies deepest in my soul, at least that of it which is communicable to another person. I have started by stating my position from the side of knowledge, now let me state it also from another side. My experience, especially that gained by repeated residences at the university, had taught me beyond a doubt that the method of education hitherto in use, especially where it involved learning by rote, and where it looked at subjects simply from the outside

---

Theodor Froebel, the third son, became a landscape gardener in Zürich, where he still lives. His son has succeeded him. One of us (E. M.) visiting Herr Beust's school there, in 1887, spoke with little "Ferdinand Froebel," grandson of Theodor.

or historically, and considered then capable of apprehension by mere exercise work, dulled the edge of all high true attainment, of all real mental insight, of all genuine progress in scientific culture, of self-contemplation, and thus of all real knowledge, and of the acquisition of truth through knowledge. I might almost go further, and say that its tendency was towards rendering all these worthy objects impossible.

Therefore, I was firmly convinced, as of course I still am, that the whole former educational system, even that which had received improvement, ought to be exactly reversed, and regarded from a diametrically opposite point of view—namely, that of a system of development. I answered those who kept asking what it was that I really did want after all, with this sentence : " I want the exact opposite of what now serves as educational method and as teaching-system in general." I was, and am, completely convinced, that after this fashion alone genuine knowledge and absolute truth, by right the universal possessions of mankind, shall find once again, not alone single students here and there, but the vast majority of all our true-hearted young men and of our professors spreading far and wide the elements of a noble humanised life. To bring this into a practical scheme I held to be my highest duty, a duty which I could never evade, and one which I could never shake off, since a man cannot shake off his own nature.

Our greatest teachers, even Pestalozzi himself not excepted, seemed to me too bare, too empirical,* and arbitrary, and there-

---

* Empiricism—that is, *a posteriori* investigations, based on actual facts and not *a priori* deductions from theories, or general laws, did good service before Froebel's time, and will do good service yet, Froebel notwithstanding. In Froebel's time the limits Kant so truly set to the human understanding were overstepped on every side ; Fichte, Schelling, and Hegel were teaching, and the latter especially had an overpowering influence upon all science. Every one constructed a philosophy of the universe out of his own brain. Krause, the recipient of this letter, never attained to very great influence, though had he been in Hegel's chair he might perhaps have wielded Hegel's authority, and there was for a long time a great likelihood of his appointment. Meanwhile he reconstructed the university at Göttingen. Even practical students of Nature, such as Oken, did homage to the general tendency which had absorbed all the eager spirits of the vanguard of human advancement, amongst them Froebel

fore not sufficiently scientific in their principles—that is, not sufficiently led by the laws of our being ; they seemed to me in no wise to recognise the Divine element in science, to feel its worth, and to cherish it. Therefore I thought and hoped, with the courage and inexperience of youth, that all scientific and learned men, that the universities, in one word, would immediately recognise the purport of my efforts, and would strive with all their might to encourage me by word and deed.

In this I was egregiously mistaken; nevertheless I am not ashamed of the error. But few persons raised their voices for me or against me ; and, indeed, your article in the *Isis* is the single sun-ray which really generously warmed and enlightened my life and lifework. Enough ! the Universities paid no heed to the simple schoolmaster.* As to the "able editors," they, in their reviews, thought very differently from me ; but why should I trouble myself further with remembering their performances, which were written simply with the object of degrading me and my work ? They never succeeded in shaking my convictions in the least.

---

himself. We see how firmly set Froebel was against experience-teaching, *a posteriori* work, or, as he calls it, empiricism. The Kantist, Arthur Schopenhauer, was not listened to, and dwelt apart, devouring his heart in bitter silence ; breaking out at last with the dreary creed of Pessimism.

* Froebel is here hardly fair. How should people know much of him as yet ? He had at this time written the following works :—(1) "On the Universal German Educational Institute of Rudolstadt" (1822) ; (2) "Continuation of the Account of the Universal German Educational Institute at Keilhau " (1823) ; (3) "Christmas at Keilhau : a Christmas Gift to the Parents of the Pupils at Keilhau, to the Friends and the Members of the Institute " (1824) ; (4) "The Menscheñ Erziehung," the full title of which was "The Education of Man : The Art of Education, Instruction, and Teaching, as attempted to be realised at the Universal Educational Institute at Keilhau, set forth by the Originator, Founder, and Principal of the Institute, Friedrich Froebel " (1826), never completed ; (5) *Family Weekly Journal of Education for Self-culture and the Training of Others*, edited by Friedrich Froebel, Leipzig and Keilhau. But Froebel, in his unbusiness-like way, published all these productions privately. They came out of course under every disadvantage, and could only reach the hands of learned persons, and those to whom they were really of interest, by the merest chance. Further, Froebel, as has already abundantly appeared, was but a poor author. His stiff, turgid style makes

! regard the simple course of development, proceeding from analysis to synthesis, which characterises pure reasoned thought, as also the natural course of the development of every human being. Such a course of development, exactly opposite to the path taken by the old-fashioned methods of education, I now see mankind about to enter upon ; nay, it has been actually entered upon already in a few single cases, though these cases are almost unknown and therefore unregarded ; and with this new course of development a new period is to begin, a new age for all mankind, and therefore in the higher inner sense a new world ; a world, perceiving and understanding, perceived and understood ; a world of crystal clearness, creating an altogether new life for science, and carrying onward therefore the true science, that is, the science of being, and all that is founded upon this and conditioned by this.*

I may image forth the position of my educational establishment with regard to the universities, under the figure of family life.

In a healthily constituted family it is the mother who first cares for, watches over, and develops the child, teaches him to " read, mark, learn, and inwardly digest," deriving everything she teaches from its central unity, and gathering up her teaching into that unity again.

The father receives his son from the hand and the heart of the

---

his works in many places most difficult to understand, as the present translators have found to their cost, and he was therefore practically unreadable to the general public. In his usual self-absorbed fashion, he did not perceive these deficiencies of his, nor could he be got to see the folly of private publication. Indeed, on the contrary, he dreamed of fabulous sums which one day he was to realise by the sale of his works. It is needless to add that the event proved very much the reverse. As to criticism, it was particularly the " able editor ' Harnisch who pulled to pieces the " Menschen Erziehung " so pitilessly on its appearance, and who is probably here referred to.

* This passage may serve as a sufficient illustration of Froebel's metaphysical way of looking at his subject. It is scarcely our habit at the present day to regard the science of Being (ontology) as a science at all, since it is utterly incapable of verification ; but it is not difficult to trace the important truth really held by Froebel even through the somewhat perplexing folds of scholastic philosophy in which he has clothed it.

mother ; with his soul already full of true active life, of desire for the knowledge of causes and effects, for the understanding of the whole and its ramifications ; with his mind open to the truth and his eyes to the light, and with a perpetually nourished yearning for creative activity, able to observe while building up, and to recognise while taking apart ; such in himself and his surroundings, always active, creative, full of thought and endeavour, does the father receive his son in his home, to train and teach him for the wider life outside. Thus should it be with my educational institute and the universities ; as regards the growth and development of man I only desire to take the place of the silently working, tenderly cherishing mother.

The life, the will, the understanding, these three must form the common chord or triad of the harmony of human life, now one tone, now another, now two of the three, rising powerfully above the rest. But where these tones are separate and inharmonious there they work to discord, as we see but too clearly in daily life :—

"Wrestling with life and with death, suspended between them we hang."

In whatever family this chord is from the first set sweetly in tune, its pure concords uniting to form the fundamental harmony of existence, there all the hobgoblins of ordinary life, which even yet often unite to annoy us, will be driven far away, there will joy and peace perpetually inhabit, there will heaven descend to earth and earth rise up to heaven ; to a heaven, moreover, as full of contentment, as responsive to every yearning of the soul as ever the Church has painted.

But since all true and earnest life must arise from and return to the ideal life, to life in itself, so must a school of development, which is to lead men, by means of their ordinary life, towards that higher life, be itself a true school of religious training in the most comprehensive sense of the word.

Man ought not to be contented with teaching merely directed to satisfy his needs as a child of earth, but must demand and receive from education a true foundation, a creative, satisfying preparation for all the grades of development of nature and the world which mankind encounters, and for the everlasting here and beyond of each new moment of existence, for the everlasting rest, the everlasting activity, the everlasting life in God.

As, however, it is only as a Christian, be he consciously or unconsciously so, baptised or unbaptised, taking the Christian name or rejecting it, that he can think and act after this fashion, you can see at once the reason why my system of education feels itself to be, and in fact claims to be, an education after the true spirit, and following the precepts of Jesus Christ.

Through love, mutual faith, and a common aim towards acquiring, manifesting, and acting out knowledge, there has grown up round me a little company of men bound together by beautiful human bonds, the like of which you would with difficulty find elsewhere. In your last letter you desired to have some account of these friends and members of my household. I will describe them for you.

But if my account is to be anything more than a lifeless list of names, and if, though it cannot be the closely-branched tree of life which actually exists, it is at least to come as near it as a garland or a nosegay to the tree, you must permit me to go back a little into my past life ; for out of the self-same spirit, whence arose my own endeavours and which gave its direction to my own life, arose also the circle of those friends who are now so closely united with me.

The German war of 1813, in which so much seed-corn was sowed that perhaps only the smaller part of it has yet sprung up, to say nothing of blossoming and fruitage, sowed also the seed whence sprang the first beginnings of our association, and of our harmonious circle. In April 1813 Jahn led me and other Berlin students to meet my future comrades in arms, Lützow's " Black Troop ; " we went from Berlin to Dresden, and thence for the most part to Leipzig. On this march Jahn made me acquainted before we reached Meissen with another Berlin student, Heinrich Langethal, of Erfurt, as a fellow-countryman of mine; and Langethal introduced me to his friend and fellow-student in theology, Middendorff, of Brechten, near Dortmund.[*]

A wonderfully lovely spring evening spent together by the

---

friendly shores of Elbe, and a visit to the magnificent Cathedral of Meissen, brought me nearer to these and other comrades; but it was the pleasant banks of Havel at Havelberg, the charming situation of the grand cathedral, the "Rhine Travels" of Georg Forster, a common love for nature, and above all a common eager yearning for higher culture that bound us three for ever together.*

The war in all its exhilaration and depression, its privation and pleasure, its transient and its permanent aspects, flowed on; sometimes nearer to us, sometimes further away. In August 1814 I was released from service, and returned to Berlin, there to enter upon the post † at the University Museum, which I have already mentioned.

Soon after, quite unexpectedly, I ran against my friends again, who had come back to Berlin to finish their studies. After being somewhat separated by the nature of our work, they as eagerly studying theology as I did natural science, our common need and inner aspiration brought us once more together. They had taken some private teaching, and were frequently driven to seek my counsel and instruction by the difficulties of their new position. When the war broke out afresh in 1815, Middendorff had been living for several months previously with me as room companion. Thus had life thrown us closely together, so that I could see each one exactly as he was, in all his individuality, with his qualities and his deficiencies, with what he could contribute, and what he would have to receive from others.

In October 1816 I left my post, and quitted Berlin, without as yet confiding to any one exactly what outward aim I had in view, simply saying that I would write and give some account of myself as soon as I had found what I set out to seek. In November of the same year my dearly loved brother,‡ the eldest now living, whom I made my confidant so far as that was possible, and who was at that time a manufacturer at Osterode in the Harz district, gave me his two sons to educate. They were his only sons, though

---

* These events and situations are fully set forth in the letter to the Duke of Meiningen, *ante*.

† As mineralogist.

‡ Christian Ludwig Froebel.

not his only children ; two boys of six and eight years old
respectively. With these boys I set out for a village on the Ilm
called Griesheim, and there I added to my little family, first two,
then a third, that is, altogether three other nephews, the orphan sons
of my late dearest brother,* he who had always best sympathised
with me through life. He had been minister at Griesheim, and
his widow still lived there. He had died of hospital fever in
1813, just after the cessation of the war. I reckon, therefore, the
duration of my present educational work from November 16th,
1816.

Already I had written from Osterode to Middendorff at Berlin,
inviting him and Langethal to join me and help in working out
a system of life and education worthy of *man*. It was only
possible for Middendorff to reach me by April 1817, and
Langethal could not arrive until even the following September.
The latter, however, sent me, by Middendorff, his brother, a boy
of eleven years old ; † so that I now had six pupils. In June of
the same year (1817) family reasons caused me to move from
Griesheim to this place, Keilhau.‡ Next came other pupils also,
with Langethal's arrival in September. My household was
growing fast, and yet I had no house of my own. In a way only
comprehensible to Him Who knows the workings of the mind, I
managed by November to get the school that I now occupy built
as a frame-house, but without being in possession of the ground
it stood on.

I pass over the space of a year, which was nevertheless so rich
in experiences of trouble and joy, of times when we were cast
down, and other times when we were lifted up, that its description
would easily fill many times the space even of this long letter.
In June of the following year I became in the most remarkable
way possessor of the little farm which I still hold, in Keilhau, and
thus for the first time possessor also of the land upon which the

---

* Christoph.

† This younger Langethal afterwards became a Professor in the University
of Jena.

‡ The minister's widow lost her widow's privilege of residence at Griesheim
on the death of her father, and bought a farm at Keilhau.

schoolhouse had already been erected.*   As yet there were no other buildings there.

In September 1818 I brought to the household, still further increased, and now so rich with children and brothers, its *housewife,* in the person of a lady whom a like love of Nature and of childhood with my own, and a like high and earnest conception of education, as the preparation for a life worthy of man, had drawn towards me.   She was accompanied by a young girl whom she had some time before adopted as a daughter, and who now came with her to assist her in the duties of the household.†

We had now a severe struggle for existence for the whole time up to 1820.   With all our efforts we never could get the school house enlarged ; other still more necessary buildings had to be erected first, under pressing need for them. ‡   In the year 1820,

---

* Froebel told his sister-in-law that he " desired to be a father to her orphaned children." The widow understood this in quite a special and peculiar sense, whereof Froebel had not the remotest idea. Later on, when she came to know that Froebel was engaged to another lady, she made over to him the Keilhau farm, and herself went to live at Volkstädt.

† This young girl, the adopted daughter of the first Madame Froebel, was named Ernestine Chrispine, and afterwards married Langethal. Froebel's first wife, Henrietta Wilhelmine Hoffmeister, was born at Berlin 20th September, 1780, and was therefore thirty-eight at the time of her marriage. She was a remarkable woman, highly cultured, a pupil of Schleiermacher and of Fichte. Before her marriage with Froebel she had been married to an official in the War Office, and had been separated from him on account of his misconduct. Middendorff and Langethal knew the family well, and had frequently spoken with Froebel about this lady, who was admired and respected by both of them. Froebel saw her once in the mineralogical museum at Berlin, and was wonder-fully struck by her, especially because of the readiness in which she entered into his educational ideas. When afterwards he desired to marry, he wrote to the lady and invited her to give up her life to the furtherance of those ideas with which she had once shown herself to be so deeply penetrated, and to become his wife. She received his proposal favourably, but her father, an old War Office official, at first made objections. Eventually she left her comfortable home to plunge amidst the privations and hardships of all kinds abundantly connected with educational struggles. She soon rose to great honour with all the little circle, and was deeply loved and most tenderly treated by Froebel himself. In her willingness to make sacrifices and her cheerfulness under privations, she set them all an example. She died at Blankenburg in May 1839.

‡ The expected dowry was never forthcoming, which made matters harder.

on Ascension Day, my brother from Osterode, whose two sons
were already my pupils, came to join me with his whole family
and all his possessions; urged by his love for his boys, and a wish to
help in the advancement of my life's purpose.   As my brother,
beyond the two sons I have mentioned, had three daughters, my
family was increased by five persons through his arrival. *

The completion of the school-house was now pushed on with
zeal; but it was 1822 before we got it finished.   Our life from
this point becomes so complex that it is impossible to do more
than just mention what applies to the Association formed by
our still united members.

In 1823, Middendorff's sister's son Barop, till then a divinity
student in Halle, visited us; and he was so impressed by the
whole work that he was irresistibly driven soon afterwards to join
us in our life-task.†   Since 1823, with the exception of such breaks
as his work in life demanded, he has been uninterruptedly one of
our community, sharing in our work.   At this moment ‡ he is in
Berlin, serving his one year with the colours as a volunteer, and
devoting what time he has to spare, to earnest study, especially
that of natural science.   We hope to have him back with us next
spring.   In the autumn of 1825 Langethal became engaged to my
wife's adopted daughter, who had come with her from Berlin ;
and Middendorff became engaged to my brother's eldest daughter.
Ascension Day 1826 was the wedding-day for both couples.
Heaven blessed each marriage with a daughter, but took back to
itself the little one of Langethal.

Still another faithful colleague must I remember here, Herr
Carl from Hildburghausen, who has been since New Year's

---

* Christian had already assisted his brother at Griesheim, and before that, to
the utmost of his power.   The three daughters were (1) Albertine, born 29th
December, 1801, afterwards married Middendorff; (2) Emilie, born 11th
July, 1804, married Barop, died 18th August, 1860, at Keilhau ; (3) Elise,
born 5th January, 1814, married Dr. Siegfried Schaffner, one of the Keilhau
colleagues, later on.

† Johannes Arnold Barop, Middendorff's nephew, was born at Dortmund,
29th November, 1802.   He afterwards became proprietor and principal of
Keilhau.

‡ March 1828.

Day 1825 a member of our Institute, his particular work being to teach instrumental music and singing. He lives and works in the true spirit of the Institute, and is bound up heart and soul with its fortunes.* Of other teachers, who have assisted us in the Institute for greater or less time, I need not speak ; they never properly belonged to our circle. Amongst all the specially associated members of our little band, not one breach has occurred since the beginning of our work. I would I could feel that I had accomplished what I have aimed at in this letter— namely, to make you acquainted with the inner deep-seated common life which really binds together the members composing our outwardly united association ; although it has only been feasible rather to suggest by implication the internal mental phenomena of the external bonds of union than properly to indicate them and to set them clearly forth.

* * * * * * *

* This excellent man was drowned in the Saale while bathing, soon after this letter was written.

This ends the autobiographical part of the Krause letter. Here and there in the footnotes the present editors, profound admirers of the great master, have ventured to criticise frankly the inordinate belief in himself which was at once Froebel's strength and his weakness. On the one hand, his noble and truly gigantic efforts were only made possible by his almost fanatical conviction in his principles and in his mission. On the other hand, this dogmatic attitude made it very difficult to work with him, for persons of any independence of mind. He could scarcely brook discussion, never contradiction. This is most characteristically shown by a fragment of Froebel's dated 1st April, 1829, as follows :—

" I consider my own work and effort as *unique* in all time, as *necessary* in itself, and as the *messenger of reformation* for all ages, working forwards and backwards, offering and giving to mankind all that it needs, and all that it perpetually seeks on every side. I have no complaint to make if others think otherwise about it ; I can bear with them ;* I can even, if need be, live with them, and this I have actually done ; but I can share no life-aim with them, they and I have no *unity* of purpose in life. It is not I, it is they who are at fault herein ; I do not separate myself from them, they withdraw themselves from me."

To get a view of Froebel's work from the practical side, so as to supplement the account we have received from Froebel himself as to the origination and development of the principles upon which that work was based, we have selected a sketch by Barop entitled "Critical Moments in the Froebel Community ;" written for Dr. Lange's edition by Barop (then the principal and proprietor of Keilhau) about the year 1862.

---

* He always regarded himself as perfectly tolerant.

CRITICAL MOMENTS IN THE FROEBEL COMMUNITY.

UNDER this heading Barop writes as follows :—

About 1827 we were in an unusually critical position. You know how little means we had when we began to create our Institution.* Middendorff had sacrificed his entire inheritance from his father, but the purchase of the ground and the erection of necessary buildings called for considerable sums, so that Middendorff's addition to the capital had disappeared like drops of water falling on a hot stone. My father-in-law, Christian Ludwig Froebel, had later on come forward and placed his entire fortune unconditionally in the hands of his brother,† but even this sacrifice was not sufficient to keep away care and want from the door. My own father was a man of means, but he was so angry at my joining the Froebel community at Keilhau ‡ that he refused me any assistance whatever. Mistrust surrounded us on all sides in these early years of our work ; open and concealed enmities assailed us both from near and far, and sought to embitter our lot and to nip our efforts in the bud. None the less for this, the institution blossomed quick and fair ; but later on, through the well-known persecution directed against associations of students, it was brought to the verge of ruin, for the spirit of 1815 was incarnate within it, and it was this spirit which at the time (about 1827) was the object of the extremest irritation.§   It

---

* Froebel moved from Griesheim to Keilhau in 1817.

† In 1820.

‡ It was in 1828 that Barop formally and definitely joined the Froebel community.

§ The long turmoil of the Napoleonic wars, the outcome of the French Revolution, ceased in 1815 : and the minds of the students and the other youths of the country, set free from this terrible struggle for liberty, turned towards the

would carry me too far were I to attempt to give a complete account of these things. At times it really seemed as if the devil himself must be let loose against us. The number of our pupils sank to five or six, and as the small receipts dwindled more and more, so did the burden of debt rise higher and higher till it reached a giddy height. Creditors stormed at us from every side, urged on by lawyers who imbrued their hands in our misery. Froebel would run out at the back door and escape amongst the hills whenever dunning creditors appeared. Middendorff, and he alone, generally succeeded in quieting them, a feat which might seem incredible to all but those who have known the fascination of Middendorff's address. Sometimes quite moving scenes occurred, full of forbearance, trustfulness, and noble sentiment, on the part of workmen who had come to ask us for their money. A locksmith, for instance, was strongly advised by his lawyer to " bring an action against the scamps," from whom no money was to be got, and who were evidently on the point of failure. The locksmith indignantly repudiated the insult thus levelled against us, and replied shortly that he had rather lose his hard-earned money than hold a doubt as to our honourable conduct, and that nothing was further from his thoughts than to increase our troubles. Ah ! and these troubles were hard to bear, for Middendorff had already married, and I followed his example. When I proposed for my wife, my future father-in-law and mother-in-law * said, " You surely will not remain longer in Keilhau ? " I answered, " Yes ! I do intend to remain here. The idea for which we live seems to me to be in harmony with the spirit of the age, and also of deep importance in itself; and I have no doubt but that men will come to believe in us because of our right understanding of this idea, in the same way that we ourselves believe in the invisible." As a matter of fact, none of us have ever swerved one instant from the fullest belief in our educational mission, and the most critical dilemma in the times we have

---

reformation of their own country. Many associations were formed : perhaps here and there wild talk was indulged in. The Government grew alarmed, and though the students had invariably acted with perfect legality, all their associations were dispersed and forbidden.

* Christian Froebel and his wife.

passed through has never revealed one single wavering soul in this little valley.

When our distress had risen to its highest pitch, a new and unexpected prospect suddenly revealed itself.* Several very influential friends of ours spoke to the Duke of Meiningen of our work. He summoned Froebel to him, and made inquiries as to his plans for the future. Froebel laid before him a plan for an educational institute,† complete in every particular, which we had all worked at in common to draw up, in which not only the ordinary "learned" branches of education but also handicrafts, such as carpentering, weaving, bookbinding, tilling the ground and so on were used as means of culture. During half the school hours studies were to be pursued, and the other half was to be occupied by handiwork of one kind or another. This work was to give opportunities for direct instruction; and above all it was so planned as to excite in the mind of the child a necessity for explanations as well as to gratify his desire for creativeness and for practical usefulness. The awakening of this eager desire for learning and creative activity, was one of the fundamental thoughts of Friedrich Froebel's mind. The object-teaching of Pestalozzi seemed to him not to go far enough; and he was always seeking to regard man not only as a receptive being, but a creative, and especially as a productive one. We never could work out our ideas in Keilhau satisfactorily, because we could not procure efficient technical teaching; and before all things we wanted the pupils themselves. But now by the help of the Duke of Meiningen our keenest hopes seemed on the point of gratification. The working out of the plan spoken of above, led us to many practical constructions in which already lay the elements of the future Kindergarten occupations. These models are now scattered far and wide, and indeed are for the most part lost; but the written plan has been preserved.

The Duke of Meiningen was much pleased with Froebel's explanations of this plan, and with the complete and open-hearted

---

* This was 1827-29.

† This is the interesting plan of the Public Educational Institution and Orphanage in Helba, with which admirers of Froebel are probably already well acquainted. It is given in full in Lange's "Froebel," vol. i., p. 401.

9

way in which everything was laid before him. A proposition
was now made that Froebel should receive the estate of Helba
with thirty acres of land, and a yearly subsidy of 1,000 florins.*
In passing it may be noticed that Froebel was consulted by the
duke as to the education of the hereditary prince. Froebel at
once said outright that no good would be done for the future ruler
if he were not brought up in the society of other boys. The duke
came to his opinion, and the prince was actually so taught and
brought up.

When Froebel came back from Meiningen† the whole community was naturally overjoyed; but their joy did not last very
long. A man of high station in Meiningen who was accustomed
to exercise a sort of dictatorship in educational matters, as he
was the right-hand man of the prince in such things, a man also
who had earned an honourable place in literature (of which no
one surely would seek to deprive him), feared much lest the
elevation of Froebel should injure his own influence. We were
therefore, all of a sudden, once again assailed with the meanest and
most detestable charges, to which our unfortunate position at
Keilhau lent a convenient handle. The duke received secret
warnings against us. He began to waver, and in a temporising
way sent again to Froebel, proposing that he should first try a pro-
visional establishment of twenty pupils as an experiment. Froebel
saw the intention in the duke's mind, and was thrown out of
humour at once; for when he suspected mistrust he lost all
hope, and immediately cast from his mind what a few hours
before had so warmly encouraged him. Therefore Froebel
at once broke off all negotiations, and set out for Frankfurt,
to discuss the work at Keilhau with his friends; since after
so many troubles he had almost begun to lose faith in himself. Here by chance he met the well-known musical composer
Schnyder, from Wartensee. He told this gentleman of the events
which had just occurred, talked to him of his plans and of our
work at Keilhau, and exercised upon him that overpowering
influence which is the peculiar property of creative minds,

* Say £100.
† In 1829.

Schnyder saw the value of his efforts, and begged him to set up an educational establishment in his castle on the Wartensee, in Switzerland.* Froebel hurriedly seized with joy the hand thus held out to him, and at once set off for Wartensee with his nephew, my brother-in-law Ferdinand.

There Friedrich and Ferdinand Froebel had already been living and working some little time when I was asked by the rest of the community who still remained at Keilhau to go and see for myself exactly how they were getting on in Switzerland. With ten thalers † in my pocket, and in possession of one old summer coat, which I wore, and a threadbare frock-coat, which I carried over my arm, I set off on " Shanks's mare " ‡ to travel the whole way. If I were to go into details as to what I went through on that journey, I should probably run the risk of being charged with gross exaggeration. Enough, I got to my destination, and when I asked in the neighbourhood about my friends and their doings, I learned from every one that there was nothing further to say against "the heretics," than that they were heretics. A few peasant children from the neighbourhood had found their way to them, but no one came to them from any distance, as had been reckoned upon from the first by Froebel as a source of income. The ill-will of the clergy, which began to show itself immediately the institution was founded, and which became stronger as the footing of our friends grew firmer, was able to gather to itself a following sufficient to check any quick growth of our undertaking. Besides, the basis for such an establishment was not to be found at Wartensee. Schnyder had, indeed, with a generosity never too greatly to be admired and praised, made over to us his castle and all its furniture, his plate, his splendid library,—in short, all that was in or around the castle was fully at our disposition; but he would permit no new buildings or alterations of any sort, and as the rooms assigned to us were in no way suitable for our use, it was evident that his generous support must be regarded as only a temporary and passing assistance. We perceived the evil

---

* The Wartensee is a small lake in the canton Luzern, not far from Sempach.
† About 30s.
‡ Auf Schuster's Rappen,—*i.e.*, on foot. (This was in 1832.)

of our situation in all its keenness, but we saw no way out of the difficulty.

In a most remarkable way there dawned upon us a new prospect at the very moment when we least expected it. We were sitting one day in a tavern near Wartensee, and talking of our struggles with some strangers who happened to be there. Three travellers were much interested in our narrative. They gave themselves out as business people from Willisau,* and soon informed us that they had formed the notion of trying to get some assistance for us, and our enterprise for their native town. This they actually did. We received an invitation from twenty associated well-to-do families in Willisau to remove our school there, and more fully to work out our plans amongst them. The association had addressed the cantonal authorities, and a sort of castle was allotted provisionally to us. About forty pupils from the canton at once entered the school, and now we seemed at last to have found what we had so long been seeking. But the priests rose up furiously against us with a really devilish force. We even went in fear of our lives, and were often warned by kind-hearted people to turn back, when we were walking towards secluded spots, or had struck along the outlying paths amongst the mountains. To what abominable means this spirit of bigotry resorted, the following example may serve to show.

In Willisau a church festival is held once a year, in which a communion-wafer is shown, miraculously spotted with blood. The drops of blood were believed by the people to have been evoked from the figure of Jesus by the crime of two gamblers; who, having cursed Jesus, flung their sword at him, whereupon the devil appeared. As "God be with us"† seized the villains by the throat, a few drops of blood trickled from Jesus' wounds. To prevent others, therefore, from falling in a like way into the power of the arch-deceiver, a yearly commemorative festival is held at Willisau. The wafer is shown as a warning to devout

---

* A small town not far away, still in the canton Luzern.

† This was a familiar name for the devil, till a few years back, in Germany; surprisingly recalling the term "Eumenides" for the Greek Furies, since it originated in a desire to speak of so powerful an enemy in respectful terms, lest he should take offence.

people, who flock in crowds from all parts of the neighbourhood
to join in the procession which closes the ceremony. We felt of
course compelled to attend, and as we wished to take our part,
we offered to lead the singing. I feared an outbreak, and I earnestly
implored my friends to keep quiet under any circumstances, and
whatever happened, to give no pretext for any excitement. Our
singing was finished, when in the place of the expected preacher,
suddenly there appeared a blustering, fanatical Capuchin monk.
He exhausted himself in denunciations of this God-forsaken,
wicked generation, sketched in glaring colours the pains of hell
awaiting the accursed race, and then fell fiercely upon the alarmed
Willisauers, upbraiding them, as their worst sin, with the fostering
of heretics in their midst, the said "heretics" being manifestly
ourselves. Fiercer and fiercer grew his threats, coarser and
coarser his insults against us and our well-wishers, more and more
horrible his pictures of the flames of hell, into grave danger
of which the Willisauers, he said, had fallen by their awful sin.
Froebel stood as if benumbed, without moving a muscle, or
changing a feature, exactly in face of the Capuchin, in amongst
the people; and we others also looked straight before us, immov-
able. The parents of our pupils, as well as the pupils themselves,
and many others, had already fled midway in the monk's Jeremiad.
Every one expected the affair to end badly for us; and our friends,
outside the church, were taking precautions for our safety, and
concerting measures for seizing the monk who was thus inciting
the mob to riot. We stood quite still all the time in our places
listening patiently to the close of the Capuchin's tirade : "Win,
then, for yourselves an everlasting treasure in heaven," shouted
he, "bring this misery to an end, and suffer the wretched men to
remain no longer amongst you. Hunt the wolves from the land,
to the glory of God and the rage of the devil. Then will peace
and blessing return, and great joy in heaven with God, and on
earth with those who heartily serve Him and His saints. Amen."
Hardly had he uttered the last word than he disappeared through
a side door and was no more seen. As for us, we passed quietly
through the staring and threatening mob. No hand was raised
against us at that moment, but danger lay about us on every side,
and it was no pleasure to recognise the fact that the sword of

Damokles always hung by a hair over our head. Feeling very uneasy at our insecure condition, I was sent, on the part of the rest, to the authorities of the canton, especially to Abbe Girard,[*] and the mayor, Eduard Pfyffer, to beg that they would provide for our safety with all the means in their power. On my way I was recognised by a priest for one of the newly-introduced "heretics" as I rested a moment in an inn. The people there began to talk freely about me, and to cast looks of hatred and contempt at me. At last, the priest waxing bolder and bolder, accused me aloud of abominable heresy. I arose slowly, crossed with a firm step over to the black-frocked one, and asked him, "Do you know, sir, who Jesus Christ was, and do you hold Him in any particular esteem?" Quite nonplussed by my firm and quiet address he stammered out, "Certainly, He is God the Son, and we must all honour Him and believe on Him, if we are to escape everlasting damnation." I continued, "Then perhaps you can tell me whether Christ was a Catholic or a Protestant?"

The black-frock was silenced, the crowd stared, and presently began to applaud. The priest made off, and I was left in peace. My question had answered better than a long speech.

In Eduard Pfyffer I found an estimable sterling man of humane and firm character. He started from the fundamental principle that it was of little use freeing the people from this or that special superstition, but that we should do better by working for the future against sloth of thought and want of independent mental character from the very bottom—namely, by educating our young people. Therefore, he set great store by our undertaking. And when I told him of our downcast spirits and the absolute danger in which we lived at the moment, he replied :—" There is only one way to ensure your safety. You must win over the people. Work on a little longer, and then invite them all from far and near to a public examination. If this test wins over the crowd to your side, then, and only then, are you out of harm's reach." I went home, and we followed this counsel. The examination was held on a lovely day in autumn. A great crowd

---

[*] A Swiss educational writer of great power and charm. His school books, "Sur la langue maternelle," are really valuable.

from several cantons flocked together, and there appeared dele-
gates from the authorities of Zürich, of Bern, and other cantons.
Our contest with the clerical party, which had been commented
upon in most of the Swiss journals, had drawn all eyes upon us.
We scored a great victory with our examination. The children
developed so much enthusiasm, and answered so readily, that all
were agreeably surprised, and rewarded us with loud applause.
From seven in the morning till seven in the evening lasted this
examination, closing with games and gymnastic exercises performed by the whole school. We rejoiced within ourselves; for
our undertaking might now be regarded as fairly floated. The
institution was spoken of in the great Council of the Canton, and
most glowing speeches were delivered in our favour by Herr
Pfyffer, Herr Amrhyn, and others. The Council decided that the
castle and its outbuildings should be let to us at a very cheap
rate, and that the Capuchin who had openly incited to riot
against us should be expelled from the canton.

A little time after this examination a deputation from Bern
came to invite Froebel to undertake the organisation of an
Orphanage at Burgdorf. Froebel suggested that he should not
be restricted to teach orphans alone in the new establishment;
his request was granted, and he then accepted the invitation.

With this, it seemed to me, my mission in Switzerland was at
an end, and I began to long to return to Keilhau; my eldest son
was now a year old, and I had never yet seen him. Middendorff
left his family, and replaced me at Willisau, living there for four
years far away from wife and child.* At Keilhau I found things
had improved, and the numbers had increased most cheeringly. I
determined to throw all my strength into the work of raising
the mother institution from her slough of debt. I began by a
piece of honourable swindling: and borrowed of Peter to pay
Paul, covering one debt with another, but at the same time
making it appear that we were paying our way. In this fashion
our damaged credit was restored, and as the receipts grew

---

* The editors venture to call attention to these little facts as a sample of the
extraordinary devotion which Froebel knew how to inspire in his colleagues.
Barop returned to Keilhau in 1833, Middendorff went to Willisau in 1836.

happily greater and greater, I began to gain ground.   Eventually
I was able to send help to the other branches of our community,
to increase my help as time went on, and to prepare a place of
refuge for them if anything went wrong elsewhere.

In Switzerland our enterprise did not develop as rapidly as we
desired, in spite of the sanction of the Council of the Canton.
The institution at Willisau gained unlimited confidence there ; but
the malevolent opposition of the clerical party secretly flourished
as before, and succeeded in depriving it of all aid from more
distant places.   Under these circumstances we could not attain
that prosperity which so much activity and self-sacrificing work
on the part of our circle must otherwise infallibly have brought.

Ferdinand Froebel and Middendorff remained in Willisau.
Froebel and his wife went to Burgdorf, to found and direct the
proposed Orphanage.*   In his capacity as Director, Froebel had to
give what was called a Repetitive Course to the teachers.   In
that Canton, namely, there was an excellent regulation which
gave three months' leave to the teachers once in every two
years.†   During this leave they assembled at Burgdorf,
mutually communicated their experiences, and enriched their
culture with various studies.   Froebel had to preside over the
debates and to conduct the studies, which were pursued in
common.   His own observations and the remarks of the teachers
brought him anew to the conviction that all school education was
as yet without a proper foundation, and, therefore, that until the
education of the nursery was reformed nothing solid and worthy
could be attained.   The necessity of training gifted capable
mothers occupied his soul, and the importance of the education
of childhood's earliest years became more evident to him than
ever.   He determined to set forth fully his ideas on education,
which the tryanny of a thousand opposing circumstances had
always prevented him from working out in their completeness ;
or at all events to do this as regards the earliest years of man,
and then to win over the world of women to the actual accomplishment of his plans.   Pestalozzi's " Mothers' Book " (*Buch der*

---

* In 1833.
† This regulation is still happily in force.

Mütter) Froebel would replace by a complete theoretical and practical system for the use of women in general. An external circumstance supervened at this point to urge him onwards. His wife grew alarmingly ill, and the physicians prescribed complete absence from the sharp Swiss mountain air. Froebel asked to be permitted to resign his post, that he might retire to Berlin. The Willisau Institution, although outwardly flourishing, was limited more and more narrowly by the bigotry of the priests, and must evidently now be soon given up, since the Government had passed into the hands of the Jesuit party. Langethal and Ferdinand Froebel were nominated Directors of Burgdorf.* Middendorff rejoined his family at Keilhau. Later on, Langethal split off from the community and accepted the direction of a girls' school in Bern (that school which, after Langethal, the well-known Fröhlich conducted); but Froebel never forgave him this step. Ferdinand Froebel remained, till his sudden and early death, Director of the Orphanage at Burgdorf. A public funeral, such as has never found its equal at Burgdorf, bore witness to the amount of his great labours, and to the general appreciation of their value.

When Friedrich Froebel came back from Berlin, the idea of an institution for the education of little children had fully taken shape in his mind. I took rooms for him in the neighbouring Blankenburg.† Long did he rack his brains for a suitable name for his new scheme. Middendorff and I were one day walking to Blankenburg with him over the Steiger Pass. He kept on repeating, "Oh, if I could only think of a suitable name for my youngest born!" Blankenburg lay at our feet, and he walked moodily towards it. Suddenly he stood still as if fettered fast to the spot, and his eyes assumed a wonderful, almost refulgent, brilliancy. Then he shouted to the mountains so that it echoed to the four winds of heaven, "*Eurêka*! I have it! KINDERGARTEN shall be the name of the new Institution!"

---

* In 1836.
† Blankenburg lies on the way from Schwarzburg to Rudolstadt, about two hours' walk away from Keilhau.

HUS wrote Barop in or about the year 1862, after he had seen all his friends pass away, and had himself become prosperous and the recipient of many honours. The University of Jena made him a doctor, and the Prince of Rudolstadt created him a Councillor of Education. Froebel slept in Liebenstein, and Middendorff at the foot of the Kirschberg in Keilhau. They sowed and reaped not ; and yet to possess the privilege of sowing, was it not equivalent in itself to reaping a very great reward ? In any event, it is delightful to remember that Froebel, in the April of 1852, the year in which he died (June 21st), received public honours at the hands of the general congress of teachers held in Gotha. When he appeared that large assembly rose to greet him as one man ; and Middendorff, too, who was inseparable from Froebel, so that when one appeared the other was not far off, had before his death (in 1853) the joy of hearing a similar congress at Salzungen declare the system of Froebel to be of world-wide importance, and to merit on that account their especial consideration and their most earnest examination.

A few words on Middendorff, culled from Lange's account, may be serviceable. Middendorff was to Froebel as Aaron was to Moses. Froebel, in truth, was "slow of speech and of a slow tongue" (Exod. iv. 10), and Middendorff was "his spokesman unto the people" (v. 16). It was the latter's clearness and readiness of speech which won adherents for Froebel amongst people who neither knew him nor could understand him. In 1849 Middendorff had immense success in Hamburg ; but when Froebel came, later on, to occupy the ground thus conquered beforehand, he had to contend against much opposition, for every one missed the easy eloquence of Middendorff, which had been so convincing. Dr. Wichard Lange came to know Froebel when the latter visited Hamburg in the winter of 1849-50. At this time he spent almost every afternoon and evening with him, and held the post of editor of Froebel's *Weekly Journal*. Even after this close association with Froebel, he found himself unable thoroughly to go with the schemes for the education of little children, the Kindergarten, and with those for the training of Kindergarten teachers. " Never mind !" said Froebel, out of humour, when Lange told him this ; " if you cannot come over to my views now, you will do so in ten years' time ; but sooner or later, *come you must !*" Dr. Lange nobly fulfilled the prophecy, and the edition of Froebel's collected works (Berlin 1862), from which we derive the present text (and much of the notes), was his gift of repentance to appease the wrath of the Manes of his departed friend and master. Nor was he content with this ; but by his frequent communications to the educational journal *Die Rheinischen Blätter*, originally founded by Diesterweg, and by the Froebelian spirit which he was able to infuse into the large boys'-school which he long conducted at Hamburg, he worked for the " new education " so powerfully and so unweariedly that he must be always thankfully regarded as one of the principal adherents of the great teacher. His connection with the Froebel community was further strengthened by a most happy marriage with the daughter of Middendorff.

REMINISCENCES OF MADAME LUISE FROEBEL.

T the end of a long life, I should like to leave my reminiscences of Friedrich Froebel to his friends, so as to contribute as far as possible towards a better understanding of that noble man, believing that intimate daily intercourse is an unerring test of character, the best testimony to the whole tendency of a life. Would that I could contribute my mite towards a true appreciation of Froebel, convinced as I am that his richly endowed nature can only gradually become known, and that his devotion to the cause of human progress must win an ever-increasing number of followers !

My connection with Froebel was indirectly begun in my early childhood, because a close intimacy existed between my family and that of his brother, Christian Froebel, at Osterode. I need scarcely here remind my readers what a remarkable man Christian Froebel was ; how he showed his deep appreciation of his brother's educational effort by withdrawing his capital from his own prosperous business, to stake it all in the new school at Keilhau ; and how faithfully he remained there, through good report and evil report, even after blindness came upon him, until death closed an old man's career.

My father (Levin) was a tanner at Osterode, in the Harz Mountains ; Christian Froebel was a spinner and dyer of linen thread in the same town. His family and mine were opposite neighbours in a suburb called " Marienvorstadt." Christian Froebel was a busy man ; yet he found time for mental culture, as well as for an earnest and loving discharge of his duties as husband and father. He himself had suffered from the want of a thorough education ; and his great desire was to procure more educational advantages for his children than he himself had enjoyed.

Froebel always had great influence in this brother's family ; his nephews and nieces (and my older brothers and sisters as well) all looked forward to *Oheim's* (uncle's) visits as a treat ; he was much occupied with them, and his presence was stimulating to them all.

In 1816, when Froebel began his boys' school at Griesheim, Christian Froebel at once confided his two sons, Ferdinand and William, to their uncle's care; and in 1820 Christian removed with his whole family to Keilhau, believing he would there find for all his children a better education than Osterode could offer.

I was five years old when our dear faithful friends removed from our neighbourhood. Well do I remember my brothers' and sisters' sorrow at parting with them ; my own grief was more speedily assuaged by a legacy of all the toys left in the forsaken nursery over the way.

Mutual promises to carry on a correspondence were kept, and thus a substitute was found to fill the blank which the loss of daily intercourse had left in our family life. Keilhau became a name in our household which conjured up delightful associations in our childish imaginations. To Elise Froebel (two years my senior) I wrote letters ; but to indite these first love messages my elder sister held my baby hand. We exchanged seeds for our gardens, and we had much to tell each other about simple country pleasures.

A few years passed, and then we had the pleasure of a visit from our friends. The fine natural manliness of the Keilhau boys distinguished them from other boys : they were first in every athletic sport, and showed to our admiring gaze what could be accomplished at Keilhau. In imitation of them, my brothers made a walking tour to Thuringia some time afterwards ; and on their return they were never tired of talking about Keilhau, the El Dorado of boys, about the kindness of *Oheim* in allowing them to share in the life of the school. They brought back home-made presents for each of us, models of toys in cut and pasted card-board. All this quickened in me the desire to make a pilgrimage to that loved spot; to me it seemed from that time forward a land of promise : perhaps it was a kind of instinct that I should one day find there my future mission in life. However, I am anticipating; for as yet many a year lay between me and the goal of my existence.

I was early initiated into the sorrows of life. My father died of consumption when I was thirteen years old; other deaths followed in quick succession in my family, darkening my young existence. My two brothers, one a bookseller at Elbing, the other a lawyer at Osterode, both had the misfortune to be left widowers with families, after a few years of married happiness. My eldest sister also lost her husband in the prime of life. I thus had many opportunities of stepping into the breaches made by death in our immediate neighbourhood, and for many years it seemed to be my destiny to have others thrown upon my care.

My education was neither better nor worse than that of most girls at that time; the chief female accomplishment of the day was skill in various domestic arts. I was painfully aware of the superficiality of my knowledge. I had, however, such real pleasure in the society of children that this drove me to seek more instruction, in order that I might be able to teach them.

Although the circumstances of my early life had taught me the precariousness of all earthly happiness, I was not insusceptible to such pleasures as came in my way. I was capable of warm friendships, I enjoyed society, I revelled in the beauties of Nature, as I knew them around my home.

Thus I grew to be thirty years of age. Family circumstances changed, and I was no longer indispensable in my own immediate circle ; but my great desire was to be indispensable to some one, to fill a breach, and to have an object in life. Again my thoughts turned to Keilhau. Mme. Middendorff's hearty words of invitation, during a recent visit to us at Osterode, rung in my ear ; I determined to offer my services to the Keilhau community. I received an immediate answer, begging me to lose no time, but to come at once, and enter as a working member of the household.

The family circle had greatly increased in size meanwhile. Christian Froebel's two eldest daughters had married Froebel's assistants, Middendorff and Barop, and had children of their own; Elise, the third daughter, had just lost her intended husband by death. I was called to help in the housekeeping, in association with these three sisters and another lady, not a member of the family. Keilhau then stood at the height of prosperity; thanks to Barop's business capacity, the dark days of difficulty had been lived through.

It was in July 1845 I arrived at Keilhau, after having passed the night in the mail coach during a violent thunderstorm. I made the last stage of my long journey on foot; the valley of Schala lay before me, the summits of the hills on either side wrapped in heavy thunderclouds. Keilhau lies at the end of the valley. With a heightened pulse I neared the end of my wanderings. I received a hearty welcome as I presented myself at the door of "The Lower House," as Christian Froebel called his dwelling; and there I remained until the coffee hour in the afternoon, when I was taken by Elise Froebel to the institution, to be introduced to Barop and the other masters, and their families. When Froebel appeared later on, he came up to me seemingly in a great hurry, saying, "What an age it is since we last met!" This greeting occasioned a burst of laughter, for Froebel had evidently mistaken me for an elder sister; it was, however, argued on Froebel's side that he had really once before seen me—when I was two years old!

In friendly association with the three sisters, Mme. Middendorff, Mme. Barop, and Elise Froebel (later Mme. Schaffner), I soon felt quite at home in my duties. Froebel himself called on me a few days after my arrival. I remember he gave me much friendly counsel as to the attitude I should take up towards the different masters and pupils, and his advice proved most useful to me during my sojourn there.

At that time Froebel lived at Keilhau, but not in the institution; he rented the upper floor of a peasant's house in the immediate vicinity. His institution in Blankenburg, for the joint education of women and children (refer to his "Appeal to German Wives

and Maidens, " published in 1840*), had been closed for want of
funds, and Froebel was looking for an opportunity to start his
work afresh ; meanwhile he took pupils, when they offered themselves to him, at Keilhau, especially during the winter. These
pupils were quartered in different houses in the village, but they
had their principal meals in the institution, as well as attending
there to receive some branches of instruction. Froebel himself
took no active part in the direction of the institution ; and his
relations with Barop were strained, because he claimed pecuniary
support from the school funds, for the realisation of his ideas.
He considered this support to be his undoubted right, as he had
been the founder, and was formerly the director, of the institution.
On the other hand, his relations with Middendorff (that gifted
and faithful, yet almost too humble friend) were always of the
most intimate kind. Middendorff gave up his whole life to
Froebel's cause, and was always ready to make every sacrifice.
I often saw Froebel practising children's games with his pupils,
and I frequently overheard his conversation when visitors came
to see him. I knew little of the Kindergarten method in those
days,—that *der Oheim* (the uncle) played with the village
children was the sum total of my knowledge of the matter. The
boys' school seemed to me the most important work on earth at
that time ; and I could not understand why Froebel—the creator
of this great undertaking, the magnet which had attracted all
these people—should live apart from it all. I did not know how
much he had voluntarily resigned, both at Keilhau and in Switzerland, to devote himself to the training of women for the scientific
nurture of the dawning faculties of infancy.

During the following year, new pupils came to follow Froebel's
lessons, and amongst them a charming young lady, Anna Hesse
by name, from Annaburg.† She and I became great friends ;
she initiated me into the meaning of the Kindergarten method,
the cause which afterwards became sacred in my eyes. She

---

* See Froebel's Letters, p. 156.

† Where she founded the tenth Kindergarten in 1847. See Froebel's Letters,
list of first sixteen Kindergartens, p. 177 ; and his letter to her, p. 260.

used to repeat Froebel's lectures to me, and she gave me all her notes to read.

Froebel lived entirely for his pupils at that time; his passionate eagerness seemed to infect them. He taught them in season and out of season, when sitting in a room, when out walking, no matter when and where. As he reserved no time for himself, he used to write his numerous and long letters during the night, or during the pauses before meals. When he at length put in an appearance at the dinner table, he would seem preoccupied, and always in a hurry. Visitors often called to see him, and then he was at times very eloquent; I often listened to his expositions. One of his pupils once said to me, " Here at Keilhau you do not realise what Froebel is; you should see how he is venerated in other places!" In Mme. Middendorff's room I first saw a copy of the *Mutter- und Kose-Lieder* lying on the table. I began to read it, and soon exclaimed, "This is a singularly beautiful book!" "Yes," answered Mme. Middendorff, "it is a wonderful book, but more money has gone into the making of it than will ever come out of it again."

Looking out of the window, I saw Froebel, Middendorff, and Barop walking up and down the courtyard, engaged in earnest conversation. Froebel's face became more and more grave. Then Mme. Middendorff remarked to me, "*Der Oheim* wants more money for a long journey; Barop will not give him any." That night late, Froebel was on the road to Erfurt, in company with a man wheeling a barrow; on the barrow stood Froebel's plate-chest : the contents were pawned to raise new funds for his work. For years he paid interest upon the loan, and it was not till he was at Marienthal that he redeemed his table silver.

His journey on that occasion was to the Erzgebirge, to Marienberg, where a Kindergarten was about to be opened.[*] After a long absence he returned to Keilhau in a cheerful mood, bringing thoughtfully appropriate presents for the ladies of the household.

Both Froebel and Middendorff were at home in the art of giving

---

[*] The ninth Kindergarten, founded by Auguste Steiner in 1847. See Froebel's Letters, p. 177.

presents : they knew how to enhance the value of a trifle by appropriate words. On my birthday, Froebel gave me a little needle-book, accompanied by some verses. After supper Froebel and Elise went with me to my house in the village, where I knew that another birthday celebration awaited me. After Froebel had wished us good-night at the door, and was walking towards his own rooms, Elise said to me, " I know *der Oheim* would have liked to come in with us." For my part I had not ventured to suggest such a thing; but, emboldened by these words, I hastily lifted the finest wreaths from my table, and retraced my steps to Froebel's house. He welcomed me most pleasantly, admired the wreaths, and (as was his wont) he began to draw parallels between this and that blossom and some higher truth. The flowers were all children of the spring,—anemones, violets, etc., mixed with evergreens.

During the summer of 1847, Froebel was pleased to have an opportunity of making his method known to a wider public ; and he had an exhibition of Kindergarten games at a meeting at Quetz, near Halle. As a result of this meeting, Mme. Doris Lütkens determined to add a Kindergarten to her high school for girls, at Hamburg. Middendorff's daughter, Alwine,[*] was to take charge of this Kindergarten ; but, before entering upon the duties of this important post, she had to follow Froebel's course for six months. As I now had the greatest desire to study thoroughly under Froebel, I paid a visit to my relatives, to consult them on the subject, before entering myself for the course in the autumn. During my absence, Froebel wrote a characteristic letter to me : it also touches upon events of his life at this time, and may be of interest to my readers :—

Friedrich Froebel to Luise Levin.

" 1847 { Hanover, *2nd August.* { Bremen, *4th August.*

"Much-esteemed Luise,—The dates on this letter will prove that I was anxious to express my warm thanks for your friendly letter, and my appreciation of your thoughtful care of my Arum.

---

[*] Afterwards Mme. Wichard Lange.

Yes, a human being who (like the lily) enjoys such faithful daily care could almost take it into his head to blossom twice over, and thus to breathe out thanks into the air. I am glad to think my Arum has proved grateful.

" But a child is not worse than a flower ; and what is done by a plant on the lower stage of mere existence can surely be accomplished by a child on the far higher plane of sentient life, amid awakening self-consciousness. You see, therefore, how much pleasure and gratitude are in store for you, should you decide to occupy yourself with young children. As often as I go amongst them—for example, this very day, when visiting the child-refuges [*Bewahranstalten*] here—I am cheered by the consciousness that no other occupation is capable of yielding more permanent satisfaction, for heart and head, than intercourse with the young under natural conditions of training. I desire, for your warm affections and poetic nature, the deep satisfaction of reading in the unsophisticated faces of children, the unspoken thanks that are the result of careful early training." . . .

" KEILHAU, *September* 13*th*, 1847.—Middendorff tells me you left here for Osterode, decided in your own mind to become a Kindergarten teacher, should family circumstances permit. In view of this resolve on your part, I now call your attention to some public notices in the papers. The recent explanation of my method which appeared, after the meeting at Quetz, in the *Magdeburger Zeitung*, and the still more important one which appeared in the *Allgemeine Anzeiger der Deutschen*, give a very clear idea of my method of training, by means of games and employments, and indeed of my educational method as a whole. I have felt it to be my duty to send you these articles for perusal, and you will perhaps pass them on to those who may inquire of you. This was my object in writing ; but I seize the opportunity of also thanking you for the care you have taken of my Arum during my absence. What will you say when I tell you the plant has opened another bud, to my great delight, thus reminding me of the gentle nurture it received at your hands, and serving as the bearer of a new greeting from you ! . . . Forty-six members of the Keilhau community, pupils and teachers, in three divisions, started this morning on their usual autumn walking tour, the ladies of the household accompanying them as far as the crest of the Steiger hill. They set off in health and good spirits, and those left behind are quite equal to them in this respect. . . .

"Yours obediently,

"F. FROEBEL."

I returned to Keilhau, to follow Froebel's course of training, during the winter of 1847—1848, in company with Alwine Middendorff. I felt myself in a new world under Froebel's instruction ; it was highly stimulating.

Middendorff was generally present at these lectures, and wrote down everything Froebel said. I was allowed to read these notes afterwards, which was a great help to me, as my companion Alwine was a much more apt pupil than I was, and also had enjoyed Froebel's teaching from her childhood. The simplest event, a familiar natural process or object, a walk, served Froebel as a starting-point, a theme for a lesson. On one occasion, a birthday wreath served the purpose ; on another, he drew our attention to the ice flowers on the window-pane of his sitting-room ; after examining these, he remembered much more perfect specimens were to be found on the windows of the wash-house, so we adjourned to that region with him. From thence master and pupils walked up to the top of a neighbouring hill, enjoying the sight of the crisp snow sparkling in the sun, and of the frosted branches of the fir-trees. Natural phenomena such as these were used by Froebel as examples of physical laws ; and then he would go on to draw parallels between physical and mental phenomena. We had to make up at home for the time spent in this kind of intuitive instruction, because Alwine Middendorff was obliged to get through a given amount of work before Eastertide, when her duties at Hamburg were to begin. We played and practised games with the village children, generally under Middendorff's direction ; sometimes we walked to the neighbouring village of Eichfeld to play games. They consisted chiefly in the dramatic representation of the various labours of the neighbouring peasantry, or of the trades pursued in village and forest.

Froebel endured real hardships at this time, in order to raise money for the propagation of his new method. He still possessed a furnished house at Blankenburg, called the Powder Mill, where he had lived until 1845. He now sold the whole of the furniture of this house by public auction, at Rudolstadt, and used the money to further the cause he lived for. When he was in these difficulties, he seemed to shrink within himself, he was so silent; no doubt he felt the hardship of being without a settled home, after all these years of toil. At Keilhau, he lived in the most modest style; he endured physical discomfort with absolute indifference, absorbed in his one object. I had a sitting-room adjoining his; and as there was no way of heating my room, and the winter of 1847—1848 was a very severe one, I used often to sit at a separate table in his study. There I worked at the various gifts and occupations of the Kindergarten whilst Froebel was writing. I remember one day he was thus engaged when a poor little lad came from the village to see him. As Froebel immediately rose to get some picture or toy to amuse the child with, I could not help expressing my regret at the interruption. "Not so," was his prompt reply; "I cannot tell which work is the more important. This child may become a far more distinguished man than I am." He then resumed his pen, listening and responding to the prattle of the boy, as he turned the leaves of the picture book. At length the child wished to go, and Froebel rose to open the door.

Our studies were liable to other interruptions, as when we were called upon to direct Kindergarten games at different places. At these places, teachers from the neighbourhood, visitors, and parents often assembled: they were sometimes attracted and interested by what they heard and saw. I remember that Froebel devoted the Christmas holidays of 1847 to the organisation of such meetings in the district called the Thuringian Forest, preparatory to a larger gathering for the public performance of games. Froebel had promised to return to Keilhau, to keep New Year's Eve with the household; but, as usual, he was busy up to the last minute. In order to keep his promise, he started at a late hour on foot, walking over the hills in the deep snow from Sonneberg to Keilhau, where he arrived by the middle of the night at his cold, empty rooms. New Year's Eve was always kept as a beautiful traditional festival at Keilhau; during the early part of the evening, old and young joined in all kinds of games and innocent merriment; towards the end of the evening, there was a simple prayer and retrospect of the year, followed by a general shaking of hands and mutual good wishes for the New Year, as the bells rung out from the village church. At this moment, Froebel appeared upon the scene, on the above-mentioned occasion, and great was the joy of the assembled household that he had kept his promise. A table covered with Christmas gifts was quickly arranged for him in the blue room ; and I remember him chatting pleasantly about his recent journeys, telling those in Keilhau about the increased support the Kindergarten cause was receiving in different places in Thuringia, and describing new acquaintances he had made, until he at length withdrew, in the early hours of the first morning of the New Year (1848). Retiring to his own rooms, he sat up until breakfast-time, inditing a letter " To Womankind," as he afterwards told us.

About this time, the sister of a schoolmaster at Coburg paid a visit of some weeks to Keilhau; she took Froebel's lessons, and her interest and enthusiasm seemed greatly to stimulate the teacher. Froebel's lessons were particularly fine at this period.

During Lent (1848), Froebel was again travelling to the heights of the Thuringian Forest, to Schalkau, and other places. I accompanied him this time, both because I was necessary in the direction of the children's games, and because there was some prospect of my obtaining a situation there. Froebel lived at the schoolhouse at Schalkau, and a kind neighbour received me hospitably. Our afternoons were taken up with rehearsals ; and in the evenings schoolmasters from the neighbourhood used to gather round Froebel, to hear more about his educational views, and to talk over arrangements for the coming festival. From there we went to Brunn, where the vicar received us. After a week's absence, we found ourselves at Keilhau again, greatly cheered by the evident

interest which many people were now taking in Froebel's Kindergarten method. I remember distinctly our return journey to
Keilhau on that occasion. We were driving through the woods
from Sonneberg in a sledge, when we were overturned into the
snow. I also recall the evidences of public excitement in all the
villages along the route. This was during the spring of 1848.
During the following summer, Middendorff published his book on
Kindergartens, and dedicated it to the German Parliament, then
sitting at Frankfurt, as an object worthy of their earnest attention
from a national point of view. I well remember Froebel's
frequent walks to the neighbouring town of Saalfeld, during the
correction of the proof sheets; for this was a work on which the
two friends laboured conjointly.

The public meeting in the Thuringian Forest district, for which
Froebel had been preparing during the winter, never took place.
I believe the authorities would not allow it.

Meanwhile, Froebel was preparing for another public meeting
at Rudolstadt, to which schoolmasters from all parts of Germany, and many other people, were invited by him to discuss
his method of training. His object was to enlist the schoolmasters in his cause, and publicly to discuss the Kindergarten
question. Great were the preparations for this gathering; invita-
tions were sent out far and wide; suitable accommodation had to be
provided in and near the place of meeting. The children had to
be assembled from the different villages in the neighbourhood, to
learn games and rehearse gymnastic exercises. I was frequently
on my way to the little schoolhouse at Eichfeld, to show the children paper-folding and paper-cutting exercises, and lath interlacing.
Here Froebel often joined us, after having walked from Saalfeld, *via*
Rudolstadt, arousing the people's interest at each place he visited.

The following letter, addressed to me before this meeting, will
perhaps best show what hopes Froebel entertained for the spread
of his cause at this time :—

"BAUTZEN IN SILESIA, *May 29th*, 1848.

"DEAR LUISE,—Little did I think, when we parted at Schalkau,
that my next letter to you would be dated from Silesia; thus,
circumstances force us onward towards our goal, without our

knowledge or will. On arriving at Leipzig, I immediately sought information about the meeting of teachers, and found, to my dismay, that it was to take place at Oschatz. . . . As to that meeting, I report only what is important for you and for me to know,—namely, that the following resolution was put to the meeting, and carried unanimously : 'That the governments of Saxony and Meiningen be respectfully urged to make the support of Kindergartens obligatory in every parish within their dominions, as the best possible foundation upon which to rear any system of public instruction.'" . . .

The meeting at Rudolstadt, in August 1848, was an important one in the history of the Kindergarten movement, as several public men, members of the National Legislative Assembly, or of their respective governments, had been deputed to be present, to inquire into Froebel's method. Members of some of the reigning families of the Thuringian states were present during the three days' discussions, and many men of distinction took part in the deliberations. Judging from the animation of these debates, there was a strong element of opposition in the assembly. Froebel and his friends were often challenged, and they had to defend their position with all the energy and skill they could command. On the whole, Froebel's cause was greatly benefited by the discussions; for although some people may have retained intellectual doubts about some details of his method, no one went away from that meeting without warmly sympathising with his work as a whole. They could not deprive Froebel of the undoubted honour of having brought to light some neglected truths respecting child-nature, and of having provided fresh means for its development. After the meeting, Mme. Lütkens, one who was present, wrote to Middendorff, " I have reaped a splendid mental harvest at Rudolstadt ; and, God willing, its fruit shall be made manifest at Hamburg, where I hope to extend the sphere of our propaganda. Alwine's presence here (at Hamburg) has been a fortunate circumstance for the spread of the Kindergarten cause; the field is extending on every side, since all the mothers and children are now with us for love of Alwine. I am so glad to know Mdlle.

Levin [the writer of these Reminiscences] is going to Rendsburg, there to sow the good seed. Kindergartens are God's cause, therefore they must spread; and I rejoice to see how well prepared many minds find themselves for the reception of this new truth, as soon as they begin to investigate the matter. If only a great multitude had the wisdom to turn to the fountain head, to the first and oldest Kindergarten teacher, to learn of him while they may! Granted that we have been shown how the thing is to be done, no discussions will ever, in my eyes, equal Froebel's own way with children as a demonstration of the absolute harmony which exists between the nature of the child and the principles of his method; they are absolutely *one* and indissoluble: they belong together. . . . Other people reflect parts of his truth: he alone reflects the *whole* truth. . . . Hence I declare myself to be ultra-Froebelian, and look upon all those who stand shoulder to shoulder with him as but broken lights. . . . Anna Martyn says, ' The army with which our Saviour did battle and won victories was an army of women and children.' He demanded devotion and faith, hence they were the chosen ones. Why not draw the parallel between then and now? We women and children must *embody* Froebel's great message in real life: it is a truth which reveals itself more readily to the spiritual eye than to the slower instrument of reason, especially when reason permits itself to pass hasty judgment upon a new and most original personality, for that I hold Froebel undoubtedly to be. . . . Please remember me to him in grateful veneration." . . .

If the public session at Rudolstadt was satisfactory, one result was that Froebel worked now more than ever. His correspondence became very extensive; new ties once formed had to be sedulously cultivated. Expressions of sympathy flowed in upon him from very different quarters, and raised the old man's faith in the great possibilities of human nature; he had long lived through the chill of indifference and of hostility, while urging men to take upon themselves new responsibilities and new work for the sake of the young children. It seemed as if a better day were about to dawn.

Froebel received the honour of an invitation to spend the winter

1848—1849 in Dresden. During that time, an adequate salary
was guaranteed to him ; and he was to give a series of lectures
on his new method. Adolf Frankenberg (a former pupil of
Froebel's) and his wife put their Kindergarten at the disposal of the
master, in order that the students might have a field for practice.

Besides the students' lectures, Froebel held another course at
Dresden, for persons interested in his educational principles ; and
several well-known ladies and gentlemen attended these lectures.

How I wished to follow Froebel to Dresden, in company with
Henriette Breymann, his grand-niece,* whose long visit to
Keilhau in the summer had cemented our friendship ! I longed
to deepen my knowledge of his educational theory, and to be at
his side to help him, if he required my services ; but circumstances willed it otherwise. I accepted a situation as governess to
some young children in a family at Rendsburg, relatives of Mme.
Lütkens. At Christmas-time, 1848, I had the great pleasure of
seeing Froebel once more. He was spending the vacation with
dear relatives of his own at Bergedorf, near Hamburg ; and Alwine
Middendorff and I were also there. New plans teemed in his
fruitful brain ; he told us that he thought of beginning a Training
College, in association with Henriette Breymann and ourselves.
In May 1849, Froebel was at the Baths of Liebenstein, with a view
to obtaining a lease of the country house, Marienthal, from the
Duke of Meiningen. The application long waited for an answer ;
and, meanwhile, Froebel had issued prospectuses from Liebenstein,
and enrolled pupils, though he knew not for certain whether
his tenancy would be accepted. The kindly matron of the Baths,
Mme. Müller, extricated Froebel from his temporary dilemma by
putting at his disposal a suite of rooms in a farmhouse, in the
neighbourhood of Liebenstein. Here Froebel first took up his
abode with his pupils and his young grand-niece, Henriette Breymann, who kept house for him ; she also helped him with the instruction of his young lady pupils, and of some children who were
beyond the Kindergarten age. Pupils came, but they paid very
little ; and the expense of living at a fashionable watering-place was

---

* Afterwards Mme. Schrader.

comparatively high. Still Froebel was content to have a settled household once more, and he set to work with redoubled energy. He was soon the topic of conversation amongst the visitors, and was known as the elderly gentleman who taught young ladies to play with the village children. In this way, the Baroness von Marenholtz-Bülow heard of him when she visited Liebenstein. Very soon afterwards she appeared at his lectures, and from that day forth devoted her talents and her means to the spread of his cause,—a cause which she has never since deserted.

When at length a substitute was found for me, I left Rendsburg with the consent of my pupils' parents, and joined the circle at Liebenstein, in July 1849. I shared the duties of housekeeping and teaching with Henriette Breymann for a short time. She was in delicate health, and eventually accepted the invitation of relatives at Mühlhausen to visit them, with a view to restoring her health, previous to her return home. There (at Watzum), in her father's vicarage and parish, she had a rich field of educational endeavour,—instructing her brothers and sisters, and taking an active part in the training of the village children. Alwine Middendorff never joined us; she never could make up her mind to break the ties that bound her to Hamburg. Meanwhile, Froebel was repeatedly asked to visit Hamburg, and to give a course of lectures there. He decided to make Liebenstein his headquarters, but he accepted an offer to pass the winter months at Hamburg, setting off in October. I remained at Liebenstein to continue the training of the pupils, and to admit new ones. Very soon after, a Kindergarten was opened at Liebenstein by myself, as a practising field for them. We looked forward to removing to Marienthal in the spring. A busy and exciting life awaited Froebel at Hamburg. Society there was much divided on the subject of the higher education of women, and Froebel undoubtedly overtasked his strength. On the other hand, he felt strengthened and supported by the sympathy and interest his views met with during his lectures. With many aspects of the woman-question agitating the public mind at that time, he had but little sympathy; but he had the great satisfaction of seeing the first "Town Kindergarten" opened, under his fostering care, and many private Kindergartens as well.   He paid an *interim* visit to us at Liebenstein, arriving on December 23rd, 1849, just in time to be present at our Christmas gathering for the Kindergarten children.   Froebel addressed the parents in warm words of welcome; and young and old spent a few hours together, celebrating the children's festival, as is usual in Germany.   We passed the remainder of the evening with our good landlady, Mme. Müller.   The following days brought much business in their train ; one day we drove in a sledge to Meiningen, to take the necessary steps to settle the question about the lease of Marienthal.   New Year's Eve came round, and Froebel again started on his long journey to Hamburg, where he shortly after resumed his exhausting labours.   When at length he found himself at liberty to turn his back upon the great city, we had just removed to Marienthal (1850) ; and no sooner had we moved in when new pupils came.   We were all happy at the prospect of our new home.   Froebel returned from Hamburg to Keilhau, first of all, to tell our relatives there of his intention to introduce me into our new home as his wife.   This wish on our part was not to be so easily fulfilled.   It was difficult at that moment for Froebel to give the required proof that he had property enough to support his widow in the event of his death.   During his stay at Keilhau he visited Blankenburg, where he had worked so long and with such self-sacrificing effort.   The little town of Blankenburg took the opportunity to present him with the title of honorary citizen, but when he requested them to transfer the honour to his future wife they refused.   The reason of the refusal is obvious.   Froebel accepted the rebuff with his customary patience under trial, believing that hindrances were a wholesome discipline, and that help was always forthcoming when a good cause stood endangered. With the first awakening touches of spring around, Froebel arrived at Marienthal ; and we gaily decorated every doorway with an archway of green leaves, to bid him welcome.   I was painfully aware of the expression of weariness in his face.   " Oh, I shall quickly recover in this beautiful place ! " was his cheerful answer : " city life has worn me out with its excitements ; but in the rural seclusion of this place, and the simplicity of home life, I am sure to get well again."   Now followed a sweetly monotonous time of quiet work, interrupted only by walks, refreshing alike to pupils and educators, to body and mind. Froebel loved to teach even whilst in the act of walking; here he would draw our attention to the stratification of the rocks, there to a tuft of moss, or to some other plant struggling for life on a barren stone, and steadily expanding by virtue of a principle of life within. His lessons in the morning, as well as the first lesson in the afternoon, were generally given out of doors during the summer months. Towards evening groups of children put in an appearance in front of the house; they came from the neighbouring village of Schweina. Amongst them strangers generally waited. One evening a mother appeared with her little boy; they were strangers staying at the Baths of Liebenstein. The lady wished her boy to join in the children's ring, but the child very decidedly refused. I saw Froebel draw a box of the second gift out of his pocket, and walk over to the little stranger. He soon engaged his attention with the spinning toy, and after a while led him quietly by the hand, and placed him by my side in the ring. The little fellow offered no further resistance, and ever after was one of our most indefatigable little playmates. One gentleman from Liebenstein gave us singing lessons; another, Herr Koch by name, made an exchange of lessons with us: he required Froebel's instruction in his principles and methods of education, and in return he gave our pupils lessons in gymnastics. In the neighbouring village of Schweina (in our parish), visitors to the Baths often resided. One of these, a young talented teacher, Stangenberger by name, had a finely trained musical gift; he visited our house daily, being one of Froebel's most enthusiastic pupils. He inspired us with such a love of part-singing that he persuaded us to sing at a concert, given in the village church at Schweina, he playing our accompaniments on the organ. Visitors were frequent at Marienthal, and Froebel seemed to enjoy seeing people; he worked unremittingly, and seemed to take increasing pleasure in his work. At this time, the course of training lasted six months, so that old pupils left us, and new pupils entered in November. The winter half-year was quieter; and our winter evenings seemed to me particularly pleasant, the crowning event of the season being Christmas Eve (1850). I think all the pupils

who lived through that time with us would say it was never to
be forgotten. We did not disperse at that time. On Christmas
Eve we decorated Froebel's study, to make it look as if the whole
forest had moved in ; in the centre stood the family Christmas
tree ; embedded in green branches were separate tables for each
person, covered with Christmas gifts. Froebel's fatherly words
seemed to endow these presents with a higher meaning for us all.
Then came the post, bringing no less than a complete flower-
stand with flowering plants from Eisenach ; everybody had letters
from home and from friends, and thus a truly festive feeling
rested upon us all. During the following few days, we exchanged
visits with our neighbours ; and Froebel seemed to know exactly
how to give some pleasure to each one. On New Year's Eve we
were all at Liebenstein, at private theatricals ; and Froebel was
with us. After Christmas came another delightful spell of steady
work. We all felt the uplifting nature of Froebel's instruction.
Now and then we lost pupils, but they were usually those for
whom a life of such self-forgetfulness as he urged them to accept
presented no attraction.

In the meantime, Froebel worked indefatigably to bring about
our marriage. I was at rest, and entirely happy in my work for
him, and for the object he had in view. In childlike veneration
I had first of all tried to approach him in thought, and, in his
ineffable goodness of heart for the weak, Froebel had drawn out
my trust ; at length there was on both sides a desire to be legally
linked by the closest ties. His age did not trouble me at all ; in
my eyes he was the greatest and best of men, and I only
marvelled how he could condescend to care for a woman so much
beneath his level in every respect. My one anxiety was to make
sure that the rather unusual step of marriage at his age would
not do harm to his work in the world. On July 9th, 1851, when
our marriage took place, Froebel was sixty-nine, and I was thirty-
six. That day was truly a high festival of the soul for me. We
called together a few friends, and in their presence, and in the
presence of our pupils, Herr Pastor Rückert, vicar of Schweina,
asked a blessing on our union. His words seemed as if they
had been spoken out of my own heart. We did not keep a

honeymoon ; we were so happy every day of our lives we did not wish for anything more. Only the day after our marriage we spent with the guests from Keilhau, who were still with us. We took a long walk together, and on the following Sunday we drove in carts to Reinhartsbrunn, a neighbouring seat of the Duke of Coburg Gotha. There we enjoyed the loveliness of the scene, and on our return at night I remember we were all lost in admiration of the starlit expanse above us. From that time forward, we all studied astronomy ; and during that summer the star-map lay permanently spread upon a table near the open window : some of us were nightly to be found making our observations there.

The number of our pupils was large that summer. Amongst them Froebel admitted a young widow and her infant. Some of our more experienced pupils were pleased to be allowed to help in nursing the little one ; others aided me in household matters, especially when visitors came. The reigning ducal family generally took up their abode at their neighbouring country seat, the Alten-stein, during the summer months. At the gracious request of the duchess, I visited the castle twice a week, for a couple of hours, to occupy the young Princess Augusta according to Froebel's method. The little princess was then eight years of age, and showed great energy and pleasure in this kind of work. Then came a gala day, when a number of Kindergarten children from the neighbouring villages assembled, and played games in the grounds of the castle. This gathering gave great pleasure to old and young, and was long remembered as the chief *fête* of that summer.

The Kindergarten I had opened continued to be held at Liebenstein ; and in the village of Schweina we established an hour for games, in the village schoolhouse, during the winter months. The schoolmasters of the neighbourhood often visited Froebel, and every one felt on leaving that he returned richer than he came. One day, I remember, a little fellow called Joseph stood outside Froebel's study door ; the games had begun in the playroom near at hand, but the little boy would not leave his post, saying reproachfully to me, " The playmaster must come with us first." The children at Liebenstein always called Froebel the play-master, and me the playmistress. Froebel treated poor children

who came to him with great consideration; he never found fault
with their untidiness, but would quietly draw out a pocket-comb
and comb their hair for them, and tidy them with his own hands.
This kind of treatment always had an effect, for the children soon
began to tidy themselves.   Then he drew their attention to the
bright colours of the balls, and to the prettiness of clean
materials generally, and this always stimulated the children to
cleanliness.

Our happiness was suddenly obscured by a cloud, in the shape
of the famous Government prohibition of Kindergartens in Prussia.
It was issued on August 7th, 1851.   We were spending the Sunday afternoon at Liebenstein, with the Baroness von Marenholtz
Bülow, when one of the visitors present, a friend of ours, mentioned
the inexplicable fact; he had just read it in the Berlin news-
papers.   We simply did not believe it to be true, because only a
short time before we knew that some members of the Government of Prussia had expressed themselves favourably on Froebel's
work.   Herr Bormann, a member of the School Council, had
recently paid us a visit, and had afterwards published a pamphlet,
in which he had warmly advocated Froebel's principles.   Froebel
himself took the bad news very quietly, saying, " Such opposition
throws us back on our principles ; I lived through such a storm in
Switzerland, and we came out of that persecution victorious."   On
our return home, Froebel expressed himself grateful to me that I
had taken the matter so calmly ; he had a long experience of that
kind to fortify him, but with me it was different, he said : I had
only my strong faith in a good cause to uphold me.   To my mind
the prohibition was caused only by an entire misconception of his
work.   How was it possible that a Government should wish to
prohibit a work of pure benevolence and humanity ?   Had I not
experienced the blessed effects of his teaching upon the pupils he
trained ?   How well he knew how to stimulate what was good
and noble in them !   What a sway he exercised over men's minds
even at a distance from him !   I could not for one moment believe
that this error would not be acknowledged and rectified.   Now
came a time of increased activity on Froebel's part.   He forwarded
copies of every book or pamphlet he ever wrote to the Prussian

Government, along with a request for a thorough investigation of his work at Marienthal and Liebenstein. But a Minister of State is infallible, and the only answer to his appeal was that the prohibition would not be withdrawn, and Kindergartens were to be closed. The only exception I heard of was at Erfurt; I never knew how this Kindergarten managed to exist as a privileged institution. In the autumn of the same year, Froebel invited a number of people interested in education to a congress at Liebenstein, lasting from September 27th to September 29th. He wanted to lay his work before them, and to ask their judgment upon it. By the end of September, a very large number of ladies and gentlemen had responded to Froebel's call ; and they rallied round him, really to consider what steps to take for the spread of a right understanding of Froebel's principles. It was decided that a literary effort should be made, and a Kindergarten journal was started.* Froebel himself was much more mortified by the refusal of the Prussian Government to investigate his work than by its prohibition of the Kindergarten. During the winter of 1851, he seriously entertained the idea of emigrating to America. He wrote on the subject to my brother, then in Philadelphia, and sent him the outline of a scheme for opening a training college and Kindergarten there. God had willed otherwise ; and, before the answer had come from America, Froebel had passed beyond the reach of persecution to a happier field of labour.

We kept Froebel's seventieth birthday at Marienthal, as a real family festival. Middendorff came from Keilhau some days beforehand, to help our young ladies and our young lady visitors to decorate the rooms with wreaths and with growing shrubs, in pots. A fine German chorale, sung in part at his bedroom door in the early dawn, opened the day's simple ceremonial, and lifted us above the ordinary level of thought of a working day. Froebel himself was in the best of spirits, but I noticed that his strength failed him occasionally. He was, nevertheless, the life and soul of our party, and until late in the evening he was seen distributing trifles as gifts to friends. His correspondence was

---

* " Journal for Friedrich Froebel's Educational Aims " (*Zeitschrift*, etc.).

very extensive at this time; and he visited friends a good deal in Middendorff's company. I remember on one particular occasion, when Middendorff was with us, I noticed his failing strength. During Whitsuntide a great gathering of teachers took place at Gotha, and Froebel was invited to be present. A journey to Gotha was then a much more difficult thing than it is now. We hired a vehicle to drive to Wutha, the nearest railway station in those days. As we did not know the time of the train, we made sure of being in time by starting early in the morning from Marienthal. I was much gratified by Froebel's enthusiastic reception at the meeting at Gotha, and he himself spoke. Afterwards we were hospitably entertained by a friend, and I remember Froebel's enjoyment of the garden, in which we had a stroll. In the evening there was a smaller meeting; but his strength was not equal to the strain, and he hurried our departure. The weather being fine during our drive home, he stopped the carriage at the crest of the hill; and we got out and walked up the slope of the neighbouring summit,—*der Glöckli*, as we called it,—where we had often spent happy hours together. I noticed then the difficulty he had in walking, and unutterable fears filled my mind. Arrived at the top of the hill, he said, "I should somehow like my name to be placed here when I am gone." On our return to Marienthal, we found the whole house garlanded with evergreens by our pupils. Visitors called, and Froebel again became animated by their presence; but his strength was ebbing fast. The end is told by Middendorff.* He wrote under the first overwhelming impressions of those deeply sorrowful and sacred days.

---

* F. Froebel's *Ausgang aus dem Leben*, a pamphlet written by W. Middendorff, and published at Liebenstein, 1852.

CHRONOLOGICAL ABSTRACT

OF

THE PRINCIPAL EVENTS IN THE LIFE OF FROEBEL AND THE KINDERGARTEN MOVEMENT.

1746. Birth of Pestalozzi.

1770. June 24th.—Birth of Christian Ludwig Froebel.

1780. Sept. 17th.—Birth of Froebel's first wife, Henriette Wilhelmine Hoffmeister, at Berlin.

1782. April 21st.—*Birth of Friedrich August Wilhelm Froebel*, at Oberweissbach, Thuringia.

1792. Froebel is sent to Superintendent Hoffman (his mother's brother) in Stadt-Ilm.
Sept. 3rd.—Birth of Heinrich Langethal, at Erfurt.

1793. Sept. 20th.—Birth of Wilhelm Middendorff, at Brechten, near Dortmund, Westphalia.

1797. Froebel is sent to Neuhaus, in the Thuringian Forest, to learn forestry.

1799. Returns home ; goes thence to the University of Jena.

1801. Leaves Jena (having closed his student's career there with nine weeks' imprisonment for debt), and begins to study farming with a relative of his father's, near Hildburghausen.
Dec. 29th.—Birth of Middendorff's wife, Albertine Froebel, eldest daughter of Christian Froebel.

1802. Death of Froebel's father. Froebel becomes Actuary to the Forest Department of the episcopal State of Bamberg.
Nov. 29th.—Birth of Johannes Arnold Barop, at Dortmund, Westphalia.

1803. Froebel goes to Bamberg, and takes part in the governmental land-survey, Bamberg now passing to Bavaria.

1804. Becomes Secretary and Accountant first to Herr von Wöldersdorf, in Baireuth, and afterwards to Herr von Dewitz, in Gross Milchow, Mecklenburg.
July 11th.—Birth of Barop's wife, Emilie Froebel, second daughter of Christian Froebel.

1805. Death of Superintendent Hoffman. Froebel, going to study architecture at Frankfurt, is persuaded instead to become a teacher in the Model School, under Gruner. Visits Pestalozzi at Yverdon.

1807. Froebel becomes tutor to the sons of Herr von Holzhausen, near Frankfurt.

1808. Goes with his pupils to Pestalozzi, at Yverdon.

1809. Draws up an account of Pestalozzi's work for the Princess of Rudolstadt.
1810. Froebel returns from Yverdon to Frankfurt.
1811. Proceeds to the University of Göttingen, in July.
1812. Thence to the University of Berlin, in October.
1813. Enlists in Lutzow's Chasseurs (Langethal and Middendorff also serving) to resist Napoleon's invasion. His eldest brother (Christoph) dies of typhus while nursing French prisoners in hospital.
1814. Jan. 5th.—Birth of Elise Froebel (Madame Schaffner), youngest daughter of Christian Froebel.
May 30th.—Peace of Paris. In August Froebel becomes assistant professor in the Mineralogical Museum of the University of Berlin.
1815. April 15th.—Birth of Froebel's second wife, Luise Levin.
1816. Nov. 13th.—Froebel founds his "Universal German Educational Institute," in Griesheim.
1817. The school is transferred to Keilhau. Arrival of Langethal and Middendorff.
1818. Froebel marries Mlle. Henriette Wilhelmine Hoffmeister.
1820. Christian Froebel arrives at Keilhau with his wife and daughters. Froebel writes "To the German People."
1821. Froebel publishes (privately) "Principles, Aims, and Inner Life of the Universal German Educational Institute at Keilhau," and also "Aphorisms."
1822. Followed by "On German Education, especially as regards the Universal German Educational Institute at Keilhau," and "On the Universal German Educational Institute at Keilhau."
1823. Publishes "Continuation of the Account of the Universal German Educational Institute at Keilhau."
1824. And "Christmas at Keilhau."
1826. Middendorff marries Froebel's niece, Albertine, and Langethal marries Ernestine Chrispine, the adopted daughter of Madame Henriette Froebel. Froebel publishes the "Education of Man" ("Menschen-Erziehung"). Later he founds the weekly *Family Journal of Education.*
1827. Death of Pestalozzi. Froebel writes his autobiographical "Letter to the Duke of Meiningen," never completed (translated in the present work).
1828. Second autobiographical sketch in a "Letter to Krause" (translated in the present work). Barop joins Keilhau.
1829. Plan drawn up by Froebel and his friends, for the Duke of Meiningen, for a National Educational Institute at Helba.
1830. Death of Wilhelm Carl, one of the Keilhau community, by drowning in the Saale.
1831. Froebel breaks with the Duke of Meiningen, and gives up the Helba project. Goes to Frankfurt, meets the musical composer Schnyder, and accepts his offer of his castle at Wartensee, near Sempach, Luzern.
The Institution at Wartensee opened by Froebel and his nephew Ferdinand. Barop marries Emilie Froebel.
1832. Barop goes to Wartensee, and soon afterwards the school is transferred to Willisau. Luzern. Froebel at Keilhau for a short time.

1833. Madame Henriette Froebel joins her husband at Willisau. The authorities engage Froebel to lecture to young teachers at Burgdorf. Langethal replaces Barop, who returns from Willisau to Keilhau.

1835. Froebel and Madame Henriette Froebel, with Langethal, undertake the foundation of an orphanage and school for the Canton of Bern, at Burgdorf.

1836. Middendorff and Elise Froebel come from Keilhau to join Ferdinand Froebel at Willisau. Froebel writes " The New Year, 1836, demands a Renewal of Life."
Madame Henriette Froebel's health gives way, and Froebel takes his wife to Berlin. Ferdinand Froebel and Langethal succeed him at Burgdorf.

1837. Froebel begins to work out his series of gifts and occupations. Opens an Institution for the education of little children at Blankenburg.

1838. Froebel begins his *Sunday Journal* (*Sonntags-Blatt*), which continues till 1840.

1839. Froebel and Middendorff visit Dresden and found " Institution for Care of Little Children," under Adolf Frankenberg, and next year a similar school in Frankfurt, under Hochstetter and Schneider.
Death of Madame Henriette Froebel.

1840. Festival of the 400th anniversary of the invention of printing. Creation of the *Universal German Kindergarten*, at Blankenburg, as a joint-stock company. The first Kindergarten is opened in Blankenburg, June 28th, and the second at Rudolstadt, on the first Tuesday in December. Henceforward Froebel and Middendorff make frequent journeys from Keilhau to various parts of Germany to promote the Kindergarten movement.

1841. Third Kindergarten opened in January, at Gera, by Madame Schmidt, Froebel's cousin ; see Pt. II. of "Froebel's Letters," which consists of twenty letters to her on this subject.
March.—Printing of a collection of "Koseliedchen" by Froebel.

1843. Publication of Froebel's "Songs for Mothers and Nursery Songs ("Mutter- und Kose-Lieder").

1844. Fourth Kindergarten opened under Ida Seele, at Darmstadt. Froebel makes a tour for propaganda amongst the Rhine, Main, and Neckar districts.

1845.—Mlle. Luise Levin (afterwards Mme. Luise Froebel) comes to Keilhau to join her old friends, the three daughters of Christian Froebel, in the management of the household there.

1846. Fifth Kindergarten opened, at Quetz, under Pastor Hildenhagen and his sister-in-law, Amalie Krüger.

1847. Ten more Kindergartens opened : Homburg (Madame Müller), Dresden (Luise Frankenberg), Gratz, Marienberg, Annaburg, Hildburghausen, Zöblitz, Erfurt, Lünen (Marie Christ), and Gotha (Herr August Köhler).

1848. Opening of the Hamburg Kindergarten, under Alwine Middendorff, by Madame Doris Lütkens. General Congress of teachers called by Froebel at Rudolstadt. Second journey to Dresden in the autumn.

1849. Froebel settles at Liebenstein, intending to train Kindergarten teachers there, and appoints Mlle. Luise Levin directress of his training college. Fölsing's bitter pamphlet against "Froebelian Kindergartens" answered at once by Madame Doris Lütkens, in "Froebel's Kindergartens." Continuation of the controversy by the same opponents in the journal *Our Children.* Propaganda work at Hamburg, first by Middendorff, then by Froebel.

1850. Froebel returns to Liebenstein. Through the influence of Madame von Marenholtz-Bülow he receives the neighbouring country seat of Marienthal from the Duke of Meiningen for the purposes of his training college. Founds the *Weekly Journal of Education* (*Wochenschrift*, etc.), under the editorship of Wichard Lange. Elise Froebel marries Dr. Siegfried Schaffner.

1851. Jan. 9th.—Death of Christian Ludwig Froebel.
July. 9th.—Froebel's (second) marriage to Mlle. Luise Levin.
Aug. 7th.—Entire " Prohibition of the Kindergarten " in Prussia by the Education Minister, Von Raumer. Bavaria follows suit in November, so far as regards all Kindergartens except those attached to the orthodox Protestant churches.
Sept. 27th.—Meeting of friends of the Kindergarten Movement at Liebenstein. Foundation of the *Journal for Friedrich Froebel's Educational Aims* (*Zeitschrift*, etc.).

1852. April.—Froebel attends the Educational Congress at Gotha, under the presidency of Theodor Hoffman.
June 21st.—*Death of Froebel.*
College at Marienthal removed to Keilhau and placed under Middendorff, Madame Luise Froebel also assisting.

1853. Middendorff enthusiastically received by the Congress at Salzungen, when addressing it on Froebelian methods.
Nov. 27th.—*Death of Middendorff.* Keilhau under Barop; Madame Luise Froebel still remaining there.

1854. Madame Luise Froebel goes to Dresden in the spring to assist Dr. Bruno Marquardt (husband of Luise Frankenberg) in his Kindergarten and Training College ; Keilhau ceasing to be a Training College. Goes to Hamburg in the autumn as Directress of the Public Free Kindergarten, and trains teachers there. (She is still earnest in the cause ; and still resides at Hamburg, 1892.)
First Kindergarten in England, at Hampstead.
Madame von Marenholtz-Bülow begins her long series of missionary journeys in favour of the Kindergarten by coming to England, 1854-5.
Madame Ronge founds the Kindergarten in Fitzroy Square, London— the first English Kindergarten of any importance—and not long after transfers it to Miss Praetorius, herself going to Manchester to lecture, etc. The ultimate outcome of this visit was the foundation, several years later, of the Manchester Kindergarten Association, the first Kindergarten Society in England.

1855. Herr H. Hoffmann, of Hamburg, lectures in London.

1860. Aug. 18th.—Death of Madame Barop (Emilie Froebel).
Foundation of the Froebel Society of Berlin.

1861. Miss Heerwart comes to England to conduct the Kindergarten at Miss Barton's school, at Manchester, and Madame de Portugall that at Mrs. Fretwell's school, also at Manchester.

Madame von Marenholtz-Bülow founds *The Education of To-day* (*Erziehung der Gegenwart*), edited by Dr. Karl Schmidt, of Köthen.

1862. Miss Heerwart goes to Dublin ; establishes a Kindergarten.

1866. Miss Doreck (who had come to England in 1857) establishes a school with Kindergarten attached, in Kildare Gardens, London (removes in 1870 to Kensington Gardens Square).

1873. Establishment of the Pestalozzi-Froebel-House at Berlin, under Madame Schrader, by the National Kindergarten Society, Friedrichstadt, Berlin.

1874. April.—Madame Michaelis, who had been engaged in Kindergarten work in Switzerland and Italy, comes to England. Is appointed in the summer to lecture to the School Board teachers at Croydon. Founds Croydon Kindergarten with Mrs. Berry, January 1875.

Miss Heerwart becomes principal of the Stockwell Training College, under the British and Foreign School Society.

November.—*Foundation of the Froebel Society of London* by Miss Doreck (President), Miss Heerwart, Madame Michaelis, Professor Joseph Payne, and Miss Manning.

Miss Shirreff (President in 1875 and ever since), Mrs. Wm. Grey, Miss Mary Gurney, and other educationists, joined very soon after.

The London School Board appoint Miss Bishop to lecture on the Kindergarten system to their infant school-mistresses.

1876. First examination for Kindergarten teachers held by the Froebel Society. Madame de Portugall chief examiner.

1879. *Death of Langethal.* The Froebel Society founds a Training College in the autumn. (Transferred to the Maria Grey College in 1883.)

1880. May.—The Croydon Kindergarten Company is founded, with Madame Michaelis as its head-mistress.

1882. Centenary of Froebel's birth. Concert at Willis' Rooms in aid of Blankenburg Memorial Kindergarten. Soirée at Stockwell Training College. Monument at Blankenburg, erected at the cost of Madame von Marenholtz-Bülow.

1883. Foundation of the Bedford Kindergarten Company. Head-mistress, Miss Sim.

1884. January.—Dr. Wichard Lange (Middendorff's son-in-law, and editor of the standard edition of Froebel's works) died.

May.—International Exhibition at South Kensington, London, on Health and Education, at which a Kindergarten section, with an exhibition of work and materials, and with model lessons at weekly intervals, was arranged by the British and Foreign School Society, all the London Kindergartens (including Croydon) contributing.

August,—Conference on Infant Education in the Exhibition ; M. Buls of Brussels, Professor Stoy of Jena, Madame la Comtesse Dinan of Paris, and all the leading English Froebelians, taking part.

October.—Close of the section by a Conference of the Kindergarten teachers of England.

1887. June.—The Manchester Kindergarten Association joins the Froebel Society of London to create the National Froebel Union—an examining body for Kindergarten teachers and governesses. The Croydon Company was already represented on the Froebel Society's Council.

1888. March.—The Bedford Kindergarten Company joins the National Froebel Union.

The Froebel Society begins the work of testing the Kindergarten work of the London School Board by examination.

Frederick III., Emperor of Germany (son-in-law of Queen Victoria), amongst the few acts of his brief reign, grants Madame Luise Froebel a pension of 3000 marks.

1889. The Manchester Kindergarten Association withdraws from the National Froebel Union.

1890. Monument to Pestalozzi, erected by public subscription, at Yverdon. Inscribed : " To Pestalozzi, 1746—1827. He lived like a beggar, to show beggars how they ought to live like men. Saviour of the poor in Neuhof. Father of the orphans in Stanz. Founder of the popular school in Burgdorf. Educator of men in Yverdon. All for others, nothing for himself."

1891. Madame Michaelis leaves Croydon to open a Training College for Kindergarten Teachers at 11, Norland Place, Notting Hill. The Croydon Kindergarten Company dissolves, the Kindergarten passing into private hands, and the funds being distributed among the shareholders.